The Images of Jesus: Exploring the Metaphors in Matthew's Gospel

by Daniel O'Connor
and Jacques Jimenez

Winston Press/Minneapolis, MN 55403

Acknowledgment

Scripture texts used in this work are taken from the NEW AMERICAN
BIBLE, copyright © 1970, by the Confraternity of Christian Doctrine,
Washington, D.C., and are used by permission of copyright owner. All rights
reserved.

Illustrations by Tomie de Paola

For Mary, Marie, and Polly

Contents

Book of Matthew / New Torah

5 Books / Torah - Law

INFANCY   GIVING OF LAW - NEW ISRAEL

JOHN THE BAPTIST   CH 5-7   SERMON ON MOUNT   → NARRATIVE

SENDING OF 12   ←   CH 10   FOUNDATION OF CHURCH   "

CHRISTIAN RELATIONSHIP   CH 13   CH. IN THE WORLD   →   "
TO WORLD

TO EACH OTHER ←   CH 18   RELATIONSHIPS IN THE CHURCH →   "

              23·25   CH. - KINGDOM OF GOD   →   "

           CHPTRS END WITH SAME WORDS

JESUS IS NEW MOSES - FOUNDER OF NEW ISRAEL
        FULFILLS PROPHECY

METAPHOR / ANALOGY   LINGUISTIC DEVICE

KNOWLEDGE OF GOD IS TENTATIVE - NOT ABSOLUTE

STATEMENT OF KNOWING - "

EXPLICIT METAPHOR   I AM THE GOOD SHEPHERD
           THE KINGDOM OF HEAVEN IS LIKE

IMPLIED - " SERMON ON THE MOUNT JESUS IS
             LIKE MOSES - GIVING LAW

SPOKEN "
ACTED METAPHORS - LAST SUPPER

Introduction

All that is known of Jesus Christ comes from the metaphors through which
he sought to express for himself and to convey to others what life under God
was like to him. The gospels record the metaphors he spoke, many of which
were called parables. They also record those metaphors that he acted out. Some
of these were "signs" of the divine healing presence; others were various kinds
of gestures, such as a carefully-timed journey to Jerusalem, or the cleansing of
the Temple, or the withering of the fig tree, or the Last Supper, or the
crucifixion itself.

Virtually every passage of the gospels has as its core some kind of
*metaphor, that is, some kind of implied or stated comparison of one thing to
another.* In one passage the kingdom of heaven is likened to a mustard seed. In
another passage Jesus likens his own body to a temple. In another he himself,
speaking to the people from a mountain and promulgating a new law, is
implicitly being likened to Moses. In another he deliberately likens the cure of a
paralyzed man to the forgiveness of sins. And in dozens of passages he likens
God to a father, himself to a son.

Each time he creates a metaphor he does it for two purposes. On the one
hand, the metaphors are expressive; they are used to express a past or present
experience, to stimulate a like or present experience in others. On the other
hand, they are intended to operate as a new context in which one's further
thinking and acting will be worked out.

9

If these two things are so, it may justly be said that Jesus had no more urgent task in his life than to create and communicate the metaphors which summed up his experience and contained the plan of his life. For he was himself to be the ultimate metaphor, that to which it was said God would compare all other persons on the last day. Jesus created, the gospel recorded, and the reader of the gospel strives to understand metaphors which are intended for an ultimate statement about the life of people with God.

The present work is essentially a reading of the gospel of Jesus from the viewpoint of what we now know about the workings of metaphor. We shall have more to say below in these preliminary remarks about the way metaphor works. But first we should explain why we have chosen Matthew's gospel rather than one of the others or all four of them together.

The fact is that we chose Matthew before we had a clear reason for choosing him. We were convinced that a study of the metaphorical structure of any of the records of Jesus would yield real insight into his work and achievement. We felt confident of this because both the most ancient and the most modern biblical commentators seem to agree that to read the gospels is largely to read metaphor—serious, purposeful, and provocative metaphor, not just childish or merely stylistic metaphor. We were, then, interested in Jesus and interested in metaphor at the same time and felt that there were precedents suggesting that the two interests might combine.

We ourselves are not the practitioners of biblical scholarship, but we are its beneficiaries. We wanted to work from an authentic text, authentically translated, without, however, having the burden of guaranteeing its authenticity. We have therefore chosen the New American Bible version of Matthew's text; its accuracy is widely accepted. We want here to explore the received metaphors for their own sakes, taking for granted that in this version we have them in more or less pure condition. For those metaphors have been enormously powerful for dozens of generations in their ability to suggest spiritual realities and values. By entering into these metaphors people of all stations and talents have always felt ushered into a new level of experience, one beyond the world of simple and immediate experience but nevertheless somehow implied or foreshadowed there. The genius of Jesus lay in his instinctively correct choice of an image that could evoke for other people a world they could not otherwise see and could only dimly feel. We wanted to help make those metaphors and the universe they imply more available to the people of today.

But that does not explain why Matthew. To tell the plain truth, we chose Matthew mainly because his is traditionally considered to be the "first" gospel. It is not first in metaphysical or formal theological sophistication—that honor is probably John's. It is not first in chronological terms; of the gospel texts we have, that primacy probably belongs to Mark. It is certainly not first in terms of narrative charm or skill of characterization; for that, the prizes all go to Luke. And anyway, the general habit of Christendom has not been to take the gospels one by one at all, but to make a salad of all four, taking Jesus to be a combination of impressions from them all. In this sense, there is no "first" gospel. There is only "the" gospel of which there are four varying editions; these, in combination, add up to an almost complete picture.

Against any of these norms Matthew does not deserve to be called first.

Still, his gospel has always been the one that came first on the list of gospels. We entertain no assumptions about exactly what made him first in any competitive sense. He was "number one" in a purely formal, sequential sense, as mace bearers used to be in ancient processions. To us, "first" meant only that this is where the thing happens to start. Matthew is page one of the New Testament, whether he "should" be or not.

We soon, however, found a more resounding way of justifying our choice. We were interested both in Jesus and in metaphor, and Matthew seemed interested both in Jesus and in metaphor too. As is well known, his gospel is built upon a formal structure of comparisons between Jesus, the Christian Church, and the personages, institutions, and symbols of the Old Testament. His gospel is therefore essentially metaphorical (Old Testament = Jesus = Church). Unfortunately, the other three gospels, as well as all the letters of Paul, are built on exactly the same main comparisons, so Matthew is not unique at all.

Nevertheless, Matthew seemed to us somehow more deliberate, more fussy even, and more formal about his comparisons than anyone else. We noticed how scripture scholars have skillfully broken his gospel down into seven sections (seven! Sabbath number!), and how each section has to do with an aspect of the "Kingdom" (clearly a metaphor taken from the Old Testament and applied to Jesus and the Church), and how the middle five sections proceed in an order as regular and logical as an army parade. The version of this outline given in the Jerusalem Bible is as follows:

I	1:2-2:23	Birth and Childhood of Jesus
II		Promulgation of the Kingdom of Heaven
	3:1-4:25	A. Narrative Section
	5:1-7:29	B. Inaugural Sermon
III		The Preaching of the Kingdom of Heaven
	8:1-9:38	A. Narrative Section: Ten Miracles
	10:1-42	B. Sermon to the Apostles

This outline discouraged us. While it is for the most part undoubtedly accurate, it gives the impression that the "first" gospel might also be the leading candidate for the dullest. Its progress seems so plodding and its guiding ideas so conventional, why should anyone bother with it? Such a cut-and-dried presentation promises only the most accepted in-house ideas, and it seemed to us out of keeping with the originality of Jesus to reduce everything about him to something so readily defined.

But we noticed more things about this gospel than this rigid outline suggests. We noticed, for example, that Jesus the Savior was sometimes portrayed by Matthew as incredibly angry and arbitrary. We noticed that "new wine"—to which Jesus compared himself, according to Matthew—is so sour it is commercially worthless; the metaphor therefore is definitely double-edged. We noticed that the Jewish Temple, which in one passage Jesus threatened to destroy, he directly compared to himself in another. We noticed, too, that, as he went on speaking of God as his loving and provident father, he also began to say that fathers could be really insufferable people.

All of this encouraged us. It meant that Jesus—or Matthew—or both—might be capable of being interesting; that is, of being not entirely predictable. We think our suspicion has turned out to be completely justified. A study of the metaphors of the Matthew version of Jesus shows Jesus (and Matthew) to be far from predictable; to be, in fact, full of the most confounding paradoxes.

We now think that Matthew's might be "first" by a different sort of preeminence than has ever before been accorded a gospel. As John is first in loftiness, Luke in graciousness, and Mark in plainness, so Matthew may be first in paradox. Our own breakdown of the structure of this gospel, then, is based on a different idea from those conventionally held.

We attempt to follow the various stages of the development and complication of the central metaphor of Jesus' life. The essence of that metaphor is that Jesus understood God as father and himself as son. First the metaphor was established, then it was explored, and finally it was transcended:

Father and Son: Establishing the Metaphor

1.	1:1-2:23	Matthew's Images of Jesus
2.	3:1-4:25	Jesus' Image of God
3.	5:1-16	The Image of God as Guide
4.	5:17-12:50	Conflicts in the Guiding Image

Father and Son: Exploring the Metaphor

5.	13:1-16:23	Liberation vs. Confinement: Conflicts in Jesus' Images of the Kingdom
6.	16:24-26:25	Old vs. New: Conflicts in the Image of the Temple
7.	26:26-27:66	Image vs. Reality: The Failure of Jesus' Image of God

Father and Son: Transcending the Metaphor

8.	28:1-20	Jesus' New Image of God

Of course, this outline of Matthew's gospel is as dull as the one quoted above. We all stand convicted of our outlines. Our own excitement has not come from making a formal outline, but from trying to slice into Matthew's text from an entirely different angle altogether from the conventional studies—which we have borrowed from, which we respect, and which simply do not probe deeply enough.

What We Do Not Assume

Thus, for reasons both strong and flimsy we have decided to focus our attention exclusively on Matthew's gospel and have chosen as our formal point of view to study the progress of its metaphors from beginning to end.

From the outset we wish to make clear some of the things we do not consider to be involved in this task.

First, we do not assume that studying the structure and purposes of its metaphors is the only way to penetrate to the meaning of such a text. We confess happily that we think it one of the most fruitful ways we know of, but we have no intention of trying to prove that it is *the* way to do things. Such an assertion would imply, among other things, that metaphor and thought are the same thing. Indeed, some such thesis *may* be implied in what we will say below, but though we are personally tempted by it we do not propose it. This is not a book about epistemology.

Secondly, what we say about Matthew's gospel is not necessarily applicable to any other book of the Bible. Nor is anything that can be said of them necessarily transferable to him. That Matthew and John both use the metaphor of sheep does not mean that they use it in the same sense, or that one's use of it throws light on the other's. John takes the Eucharist with the utmost seriousness; it does not follow that Matthew gives it the same degree or kind of attention. From Luke's cross Jesus forgives his executioners and speaks consolingly to those crucified with him; from Matthew's cross Jesus complains first to his tormentors of his thirst and then to God about his entire predicament. Matthew's gospel is a text unto itself. The reader will do well from the beginning to confine himself to this text alone, forgetting the rest of the New Testament, and remembering from the Old only what Matthew wanted remembered. Matthew has built his own kind of integrity into his book, and we feel it must be respected. The same is true of all the other biblical authors, of course, but here we are directing our attention exclusively to Matthew.

And thirdly, just as our study of Matthew is not implicitly a study of the New Testament in general, so it is not implicitly a study of Christian dogma in general (of whatever variety). Even as early a theological formulation as Paul's doctrine of vicarious redemption can only be imposed on Matthew's book. The case is similar for virtually all the great dogmas: Trinity, Incarnation, Redemption, Grace, Sacraments. These elements may be found in Matthew in some embryonic form, but certainly not as they were to be developed by others later on with intellectual tools far different from his. Matthew has his own kind of statement to make about Jesus, and we believe it can and must be understood apart from theological elaborations which come from some viewpoint or technique other than his own.

In a word, Matthew thought in metaphors, and Jesus did the same before him. Neither thought in the abstract concepts of any school of dogmatic theology. For them, images carried the meanings. If others want to translate that meaning into the terms of Platonic or Aristotelian or Hegelian or Kantian philosophy or of Freudian or Jungian psychology—or, for that matter, of Marxian sociology—they of course can do so. The present attempt is to deal with Matthew and with Jesus as Matthew presents him, in terms of the metaphors they themselves actually used.

What We Do Assume

Having tried to extricate ourselves from unnecessary and irrelevant potential problems by these various disclaimers, we must now make clear what we *do* propose.

We propose, first, that Matthew's gospel, *like all serious religious statements*, is offered as a statement about the truth of things. It does not propose to be purely an affective statement nor purely a moral one; it presents itself as an intelligent statement made to an intelligent reader about something intelligible. To take it any other way is to reduce it to utter insignificance.

There is a problem, though, with religious statement. Religion is a way of knowing, and religious statement is a way of saying what is known. But, as its foremost practitioners have always acknowledged, religion is the knowledge of that which cannot be known, and religious statement therefore is the statement of that which cannot be stated.

Paradox again. As we shall see, Matthew is at home with it.

The point is: One can know the unknowable only tentatively, approximately —in Paul's magnificent phrase, "through a glass darkly." One can state the unstatable only roughly, remotely. Direct intelligence of things beyond intelligence is impossible. It is from this fact, of course, that has come all of the anti-intellectualism characteristic of certain forms of religious fervor. These exult in the defeat of the mind, taking that as a measure of the triumph of God. We do not join in that exultation, and do not believe that Jesus or Matthew did either. They both invested their efforts in building the kind of knowledge and making the kind of statement of which religion is positively capable. That means a knowledge that proceeds carefully by analogies or metaphors which compare the infinite and the unknown to the finite and the known. It means making statements that depend upon metaphorical images that evoke divine realities, but do not pretend to define them fully.

The religious person is, as Paul clearly realized, in the position of a child. That is, he or she knows some things but does not know most things. All the person can do is try to use the little that he or she knows about life in general as somehow a rough sketch of what he or she does not yet know about God in particular.

The first idea we assumed, then, is that religion is a way of knowing. Secondly, we assumed that its way of knowing is heavily involved with the making of metaphors between the known human world and the unknown divine one.

We make these assumptions, by the way, with such an illustrious predecessor as Thomas Aquinas, who wrote what still remains one of the finest treatises ever written on the subject of analogy as an instrument of religious thought.

We assume a third concept. It is that, while religion is a way of knowing, and while its way of knowing is deeply metaphorical, there are nevertheless quite distinct ways of relating to religious metaphors. There are essentially three ways of doing it. The first way—in the sense of the earliest and most naively spontaneous way—is to identify totally with it. This means that the believer joins himself or herself mind and heart to the symbols *without thinking of them as symbols*. They are seen and felt as reality itself. The distinction between the symbol and that which is symbolized does not exist in full consciousness for this kind of believer. This is truly and literally a child-like condition of mind, in which the knower is totally unaware of his or her own subjective distortion as well as the subjective distortion of the symbols he or she uses. For the young child, as for this kind of believer, there is no awareness of the symbolic medium which connects the knower with the known. The religious metaphors, then, do not evoke or even reflect higher realities; they are mistakenly taken *to be* the higher realities.

This condition cannot survive indefinitely any more than sheer childhood can. Another kind of intelligence develops to discredit it. The advent of the critical, rational, generally scientific mind shatters the religious universe of the naive. The metaphors of religion are identified as metaphors, that is, as products of the human imagination. Once identified as myths and metaphors, they no longer are seen as images of the divine but simply as projections of the human. The critical mind, therefore, undermines the two essential assumptions of the naive religious mind: that the symbols are the reality itself, and that the reality is God. With the zeal and overemphasis of adolescence the critical mind negates the naive one, accuses it of its illusions, discredits its enterprise, and shows religion up for what it "really" is—a subject for the immature. Thus did Plato reduce Homer, and thus did the 18th- and 19th-century critics reduce the Bible.

But the quasi-adolescent discovery of the rational and objective mind results in its own distorting excesses. To recognize that something is a symbol is not necessarily or automatically to discredit it. Plato seemed to think that he had thoroughly discredited Homer simply by pointing out that Homer's images of gods were anthropomorphic metaphors. That he *identified* the technique Homer was using is true; but the idea that by identifying it he also *reduced* it to ashes invites a good deal more reflection. The negation goes too far and must itself be negated.

This brings us to the third way of relating to religious symbolism. It is the way in which both the earlier believing naivete and the earlier denying rationality are transcended by a fuller kind of intelligence which is both capable of recognizing a metaphor *as* a metaphor and of taking it perfectly seriously *because* it is a metaphor. For this fuller kind of intelligence, to identify something as a symbol is not to embarrass it but to locate its precise kind of value.

For when we are trying to know the unknowable and to say the unsayable we have two alternatives—silence, and metaphor. Religious adults who are neither naively-believing children nor naively-denying adolescents are persons of both silence and metaphor. In silence is their failure to understand; in metaphor their limited success.

Our third assumption, then, is that to study religion's metaphors is not a way of discrediting religion's validity but of acknowledging it.

Methodological Assumptions

As guides to our study of the religious metaphors in Matthew's gospel, *we use two contemporary approaches to metaphor, one called Synectics, the other Psychosynthesis.* We believe these two approaches help to make explicit the metaphorical techniques implicit in the gospel.

Synectics originated some twenty-five years ago as a problem-solving strategy. Its key insight was that, in order to think a problem through to a successful solution, it was extremely helpful to deal with the problem indirectly rather than directly—or, more exactly, to deal with it metaphorically rather than literally. This means that, after clearly identifying one's problem or concern, the way of proceeding with it is, first, to find analogies to it, then, to explore the analogies themselves, and only after that to transfer information from the analogies back to the original question.

This, it seemed to us, was essentially what Jesus did in working out his relationship with God, as the three main headings of the outline of this book suggest. If that relationship is taken as his "problem" or central concern, his way of dealing with it was to find and explore a metaphor for it. Accordingly, the relationship between God and Jesus was redefined as the relationship of a "father" and a "son." Jesus' whole task was to work out what that metaphor implied.

Thus, in the most general way there seemed to be a similarity between the Synectics problem-solving technique and the way Jesus actually thought.

But Synectics is more specific about metaphor than that. It is based essentially on a distinction among three different kinds of metaphor. Each kind is a particular technique appropriate for a particular kind of thinking. The Synectics names for the three kinds of metaphor are "direct analogy," "personal analogy," and "compressed conflict." It seems to us that Jesus used all three, of course without calling them by those names.

Direct analogy is the simple, straightforward comparison of one thing (object, person, idea) to another. It is by comparing things to one another that we come to understand them, since making a comparison is the same thing as establishing a point of view. The importance of direct analogy as used by Synectics is that, by becoming conscious of metaphor as a basic strategy of intelligence, and by deliberately manipulating it, one can shake off the dead metaphors, the clichés, the nonproductive points of view that inhibit creative thinking. The deliberate manipulation of direct analogy, as we shall see (Chapters Five and Six especially), was one of the main techniques used by Jesus to help him rethink his own religious tradition.

The second kind of metaphor identified by Synectics is called personal analogy. It is a specialized form of direct analogy, in which one compares *oneself* to something (object, person, idea), or, vice versa, compares something to oneself. It is a matter of establishing an empathy between oneself and some other being. As used by Synectics, its purpose is not to reduce the other being to one's own point of view, but to adapt one's own point of view to that of some other being. Too frequently the analogies or empathies between oneself and another really falsify the other. An extreme example of this distorting kind of empathy is the "waltdisneyfication" of animals, that is, making animals out to be human beings in disguise. This is egocentric and distorts reality. It is a false empathy and results inevitably in a false understanding of the other. (But, as psychiatric experience has amply demonstrated, it does give a true picture of the ego; it reveals nothing about objective reality, but it reveals a great deal about subjective reality.)

The Synectics use of personal analogy is for exactly the opposite purpose. Identifying with another being is done for the purpose of entering into *its* point of view, thereby enriching and expanding one's own point of view. For example, when Jesus tells his disciples that "you are the salt of the earth," he is making a direct analogy which should more or less automatically turn into a personal analogy. If the disciples pause for a moment and in fantasy allow themselves to "be" salt, to feel its properties and activities, then they will have a very strong feeling for and understanding of what Jesus means. Jesus frequently invites his hearers to compare themselves to something or something to themselves, for the sake of expanding and deepening their own points of view through the empathy inherent in what Synectics calls personal analogy.

The third kind of metaphor identified by Synectics is called compressed conflict. Like personal analogy, it is a specialized form of direct analogy. Unlike personal analogy, however, it is thoroughly conceptual and abstract. Compressed conflict is more commonly known as paradox, and it consists of bringing directly opposite and even contradictory points of view together into a single point of view. It is the union of opposites. Acton's famous dictum is an example of it: "Power corrupts." Logically, power is the opposite of corruption. *Power* suggests vitality, force, coherence, purpose. *Corruption* suggests flabbiness, viciousness, disintegration, decay. Logic, then, would keep *power* and *corruption* in two different mental boxes. Paradox throws them into the same box, treating them as though they were the same thing. Paradox, or compressed conflict, is the limit case of metaphor, the making-equal not simply of things which are different from each other, but of things which flatly contradict each other and mutually exclude each other according to conventional ideas. The purpose of compressed conflict as used by Synectics is to go beyond the false simplicities of conventional logic (in which *power* and *corruption* are opposites) into a deeper synthesis which conventional logic cannot quite grasp but which is true nevertheless (in which *power* and *corruption* are precisely the same thing). Jesus very frequently talks paradox for just this purpose, as when he tells his audience, "Blessed are they that mourn. . . ." It will take more than workaday wisdom to grasp what he means by putting blessedness and mourning together.

Synectics, then, is a system of thinking based upon three kinds of metaphor, each of which has its own contribution to make:

Synectics Term	Common Term	Results In	Eliminates
direct analogy	comparison	new viewpoint	cliche
personal analogy	empathy	other's viewpoint	egocentric projection
compressed conflict	paradox	unconventional viewpoint	over-simplifications

We gradually came to think that the resemblances between the Synectics techniques and the way Jesus thought proved valid in more than just the very general sense that they were both metaphorical. They held good also in the very specific sense that the exact kinds of metaphor identified by Synectics were also the kinds Jesus himself used. *This book is the first sustained attempt to base a study of Jesus' words and deeds on the approach to metaphor now known as Synectics.*

The other contemporary approach to metaphor which has informed this study is called Psychosynthesis. As its name implies, its goal is to put together (synthesis) the various dimensions of physical, emotional, mental and spiritual life (psyche). The main feature of Psychosynthesis is its way of identifying what those dimensions are. The normal, waking operations of people going through the ordinary tasks of life come from what by now is universally called their "ego." One's "ego" is an organizing, *synthesizing center* or source of one's activities.

But clearly "ego" cannot be the only source or center. "I" continue to exist even when my normal public identity is asleep. There is, then, more to "me" than "ego." Moreover, the "I" who appears in dreams, daydreams, and various paranormal states is not chaotic or random. This "I" has an order to it. It is another kind of synthesizing center than is manifested in the various activities of conscious "ego." There are, then, two centers or sources, one relatively superficial, the other relatively deep. There is "ego" and there is "I." The "I" is much more flexible and varied than the "ego" because the "ego" is often composed of socially-conditioned roles or unconsciously-adopted postures which can severely limit one's available responses to other people or events. Thus, "ego" is a partial and selective manifestation of one's fuller self, and also therefore an insufficient manifestation of it. "Ego" is less than "I."

Just as the "ego" is manifested through the regular channels of professional, familial, political, and social roles, so the "I" is manifested through the archaic and mysterious images which are at work spontaneously in dreams and in early childhood, as well as in the religious literature and art of the world. The deeper organization or synthesis of psychic life occurs on the level which generally is called "mythic." The synthesis is done by means of the specific kind of metaphor called myth—that kind of metaphor which tells the tale of The Beginnings and of The Heroes. In myth are the awful meetings of Good and Evil, Time and Eternity, Chaos and Cosmos, Light and Darkness, Left and Right, Male and Female, Thesis and Antithesis, Higher and Lower, Familiar and Strange, Life and Death. Though apparently remote from the daily issues of bread and board, these are seen as the ultimate versions of our besetting problems. They are the more basic problems within our lesser problems, as the "I" is the more ultimate identity within the identity of our "ego."

Once again it seemed to us that a contemporary approach to metaphor—in this case, the approach of Psychosynthesis to those metaphors generally called myths—came very close to what Jesus was doing. He was, so to speak, doing Psychosynthesis when he undertook to identify the center of his life as something other than the superficial workaday roles in which so many of us express and dissipate our existence. He tried to organize his life around a deeper center, around the kind of synthesizing principle that cannot be spoken of except through the metaphors of the great religious myths. *We share with Psychosynthesis, and with Jesus, the conviction that mythic metaphor is preeminently the language of the deepest soul of the human person.*

We will try throughout the following exposition to refrain from reading any merely topical contemporary preoccupations back into the gospel, because for the most part we feel they would mislead rather than lead. Even so, we do not wish to push the point so hard as to obliterate a real connection between this text and ourselves. From one point of view Chaucer is ancient, from another, modern. So with the Koran, Euclid, Mozart, and Matthew. Across a gap of centuries they nevertheless are close enough to us to move us. Across the gap of contrasts there are still the comparisons, and these finally are what fascinate.

We will, then, try to adhere to what we feel are the legitimate comparisons between the world of Matthew and the world of ourselves. Those comparisons, we feel, have mainly to do with the processes by which people, then and now, think out the meaning of their lives. The specific raw material upon which thought is exercised may and does change, but thought itself is everywhere identical to itself. It always proceeds by the making, breaking, and remaking of comparisons—in something very close to the ways described by Synectics and Psychosynthesis.

Matthew may be utterly remote from us in all other considerations. In this one he is close. Metaphor is what makes us one with him and him one with us. It is the bond of humanity. There may be something more ultimate than metaphor underlying human thought, but if there is we do not know what it is. We stand by our earlier disclaimer that we do not propose here a theory of knowledge. But we add to that qualification this further qualification—that we can still be united to those who, like Matthew or Jesus, have gone before us mainly because they made metaphors to which we can still respond.

How to Use This Book

This is, therefore, a book about metaphor as much as it is a book about Matthew or Jesus. Each chapter is divided into two kinds of text which are usually intertwined. One consists of an analysis of the metaphors in Matthew's gospel, the other of exercises designed to enable the reader to share in the processes by which such metaphors are made. In one part of each chapter the reader is invited to be a spectator of the metaphorical process, in the other a participant in it. To watch metaphor and to do it—to this twofold process we invite the reader in these pages.

The first thing is a matter of reading and reflecting. It requires no equipment. The second thing is a matter of doing controlled fantasy, and may require here and there some equipment—always a pen or pencil, sometimes a few crayons, less frequently some index cards, still less frequently some music.

The text is designed with the following process in mind for each chapter, regardless of whether the reader is doing the work alone or with another person or even in a large group:

1. read the relevant section in Matthew's gospel before reading anything in the chapter of this book which comments on it;
2. read this text's analysis of Matthew's metaphors;
3. when invited to do the exercises, do not try to be analytical, but instead participate in the metaphorical process by doing the suggested exercises in the sections called "Your Turn."

We have tried to design the text so that both the analysis and the exercises could stand by themselves if one wanted them to, but we have tried equally hard to make it difficult to separate them. For we believe that the kind of thinking Matthew and Jesus did is both to be watched and to be done.

One last word: This book is for adults. We mean "adult" in the sense described above—not just one who is capable of receiving an inheritance, but one who knows the difference between a metaphor and a reality and who also knows that some realities can be approached only by means of a metaphor. Children obviously *cannot* share these assumptions with us. Others of different convictions, such as religious fundamentalists or antireligious rationalists, will not share them and consequently will find here little of interest.

Acknowledgment

We would like to express our thanks to William J. J. Gordon and Tony Poze of Synectics Education System (SES) and to Tom Yeomans of the Psychosynthesis Institute for their help at various stages of the development of this book. Our work with Bill and Tony in other applications of the SES strategies had excited in us the idea that the powerful metaphorical techniques they were perfecting might be used to make more available to the modern reader some of the great metaphors of our religious tradition. Our first attempts to use SES techniques in connection with Matthew's gospel were clumsy and uncertain, and Bill and Tony's largely adverse reaction to them helped us to realize that we would have to attempt something far more radical than we had originally thought of if we were to have anything but a glib and gimmicky product. In the long run their original skepticism has turned out to be more important to us than their undiluted enthusiasm would have been. Our thanks to them for that, and for their final reactions which have helped us to clarify the directions in the exercises. The reader who works through this book and who likes the metaphorical techniques used here can write for information about Synectics' publications to Synectics Education Systems, 121 Brattle Street, Cambridge, Massachusetts 02138.

Tom Yeomans has helped us by his many careful comments on specific exercises, and by allowing us to test many of our ideas on Psychosynthesis training groups. Tom's extraordinary sensitivity to the personal implications of one's choice of a metaphor shows up in this book in the form of those exercises which allow for maximum personal choice on the part of the reader. But it shows up in all the exercises in another way, since many of them have been tested with groups under Tom's direction. Without this indispensable testing of our ideas and techniques this whole book would be only the record of what we think *might* work. Instead, it is the record of what we know *has* worked, and we are therefore in a much better position to hope, and even to predict, that it *will* work for new readers. These readers, if they are attracted to the parts of this book which deal with what we will be calling "source thinking" and "centering," can write for more information about publications on these and related topics to The Psychosynthesis Institute, 3352 Sacramento Street, San Francisco, California 94118.

Father and Son:
Establishing the Metaphor

1. Matthew's Images for Jesus

(Matthew 1—2)

The Magi in the second chapter of Matthew's gospel are among the few pagans mentioned in the New Testament, and they are among the *very* few mentioned favorably. For Matthew, as for all the authors of the New Testament, the authentic terms of religious experience are to be found rather exclusively in the normative tradition of the Hebrew people. When it comes to understanding who Jesus Christ is and what kind of being he is, all of them, in one fashion or another, compare or contrast him to the personages, institutions, or symbols of the Old Testament. Thinking in just these analogies or contrasts is the essential intellectual style of the New Testament, no book of which was written by a person with a pagan background. When they are trying to show Jesus as the continuation or fulfillment of something in the Hebrew experience, they all work from the basic analogy:

$$
\left. \begin{array}{c} \text{something about} \\ \text{JESUS} \end{array} \right\} \quad = \quad \left\{ \begin{array}{c} \text{something in} \\ \text{OLD TESTAMENT} \end{array} \right.
$$

When they wish to point out his uniqueness within that tradition, or his character as the initiator of a radically new tradition, they reverse the analogy and make it into a contrast:

$$
\left. \begin{array}{c} \text{something about} \\ \text{JESUS} \end{array} \right\} \quad \neq \quad \left\{ \begin{array}{c} \text{something in} \\ \text{OLD TESTAMENT} \end{array} \right.
$$

Pagans have no reason to think in those terms. If they are concerned about Jesus, it is for other reasons than that he echoes or fails to echo the Hebrew Bible. In order to determine who he is and what his way of being is, pagans will compare or contrast him to something else—a cherished dream, an aspiration of the heart, an ancient story of rite, an aspect of nature. Jesus is still being defined by analogies, but the analogies are not drawn from a particular authoritative cultural and religious tradition; they are drawn from the general pool of human experience itself. The highly ethnocentric writers of the New Testament—who, moreover, had reasons of body as well as habits of mind to make them resent the pagans who chased and tortured them—did not think much of that approach. For that approach at least implies that the Old Testament is not the only valid norm for the great questions of religion. For Matthew, therefore, to give the Magi so kind a page at the beginning of his otherwise thoroughly Jewish gospel has to be considered a generous act.

It is worth pausing over this unique passage, for in it Matthew gives a sketch of what the religious person is like in general, without necessarily equating "religious" with "Hebrew" or "Christian." Indeed, the Magi were Babylonian astrologers, in all likelihood. Their taste for reading the stars to find out the fate of the human race had no equivalent in the Jewish or early Christian traditions. Yet, following their own techniques, they found Jesus.

Astrology and religion are very far from being the same thing. Yet they resemble each other in one central shared assumption: that something in the cosmos connects with something in people. Between humanity and universe there is at least the possibility of an empathy. The events of the universe— "universe" defined as the historical world by the Jews and as the astral one by the Magi—correspond to, reflect, even reveal, hidden dimensions of the life of the human race here and now. Or it might be the other way around. "Deep echoes unto deep," as one of the psalms has it. Those who strive to figure out the equivalences between humanity and cosmos are the religious men and women.

Matthew was trying to do that, and recognized his cousins in the Magi. Both he and they were looking for the ways in which the world was a metaphor for us and us for the world. The Magi were devoted to searching out the connection between what was going on above the clouds and what beneath. Their metaphor was a grand one indeed: that the stars and human beings reflected each other, shared a common fate, implied each other. If the Magi meant only that there were similarities between star movements and human events, or (as was common among the Greeks) that some constellations looked like animals or people, they would be making very superficial analogies only. But they went much further and blurred the distinction between the impersonal stars and the feelings and aspirations of human beings. For them, the stars and the feelings were part of each other. To follow a star and to follow their own hopes were therefore not two separate acts, not even two simultaneous but parallel acts; they were the same act. The movement of the stars and the movement of human beings were the same thing. Wisdom lay in looking now at one, now at the other, and feeling their equivalence.

Matthew cites the Magi so approvingly, not because of their astrological beliefs, which of course he does not share, but because by following their star they were following an image of their own hearts, and by following their hearts they found Jesus. What the stars were for them, the Hebrew Bible was for him—image of the heart, metaphor for the inner person, summary of human experience, clue to fate, self echoed back to self in a clearer language. The personal and felt equivalence between the movements of the Magi and the movements of the star is very much like the personal and felt equivalence between Matthew's hopes and those of the Old Testament. In both cases the personal analogy is intense and total: The journey of the star is our journey, the hopes of the Book are our hopes.

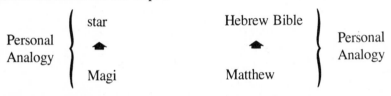

But the similarity does not end there. For the Magi the star also turns out to be the guide to Jesus, and so does the Bible for Matthew. Star and Bible are somehow like Jesus, images of him, clues to him, anticipations of him, metaphors for him. The Magi recognize the infant whom they find as the real meaning of the star—small light in a vast darkness and sole pointer of the way. And Matthew recognizes this Jesus whom he has found as the real meaning of the Book—final version of the Covenant, God-with-us.

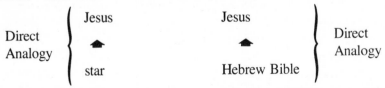

Jesus is the fulfillment of both star and Book, which in turn are images of the hopes human beings hold in their hearts. For the Magi and for Matthew, then, Jesus is the fulfillment of themselves. Indeed, they do not know their own hearts, their star, or their book until they have seen him. Thus, for both Magi and Matthew Jesus comes as the final and uniquely valid image of their own deepest selves. If, by following the star, the Magi secretly were chasing after him or, by reading his Book, Matthew secretly was searching him out, his appearance at last has the effect of clarifying themselves to themselves. The lesser metaphors become transparent as the greater shows through, and the searchers see at last where they have really invested themselves all along:

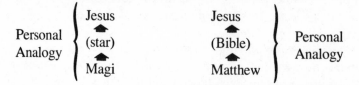

Your Turn   However generically similar Matthew and the Magi may be, the Magi nevertheless are using a specifically nonbiblical type of symbol here. Matthew, typically, tries to harmonize their symbols with those of the Old Testament by quoting Isaiah about darkness and great lights. But that does not erase the fact that the Magi are pagans and that their symbols, although they do look forward to Jesus, do not at the same time look backward to the Hebrew past. This fact makes them almost unique in Matthew's gospel. We say *almost* unique, because there is one other figure in the gospel who will use symbols not derived from or answerable to the Old Testament. That is Jesus himself.

We see here, then, direct analogies whose specific meanings are not simply to be interpreted according to a normative tradition. The analogies are free to open up new ideas for exploration. And we are free to investigate them for their latent meanings.

Our first exercise in using the metaphorical approach, then, centers appropriately on these two "free" metaphors: the star and the Magi. In the most general sense, it is clear the star is somehow the image of Jesus and the Magi are somehow the image of humanity seeking and finding Jesus. But a metaphor is not just a piece of sleight-of-hand whereby, for instance, Jesus is disguised as a star. For the metaphor to lead to new insight we must take the literal star itself seriously, consider its nature and attributes, understand it for its own sake. Only then will we be in a position to know what the metaphor of star contributes to an understanding of Jesus. The same is true of the metaphor of the Magi.

The metaphorical process, then, involves four steps:
1. knowing exactly what you want to think about—here, Jesus and the search for Jesus;
2. comparing that rather obscure thing to something better

known—here, a star and some people journeying with the help of the stars;

3. ceasing to think about the original matter directly, and instead thinking of the more familiar metaphorical version of it;

4. transferring attributes from the metaphor to the original topic of thought. It is a very strict process, and no step in it may be omitted. We would like to guide you through these steps now.

The Star

Jesus is implicitly being compared to the star. The Magi, being astrologers, believed that a cosmic phenomenon had a literal counterpart on earth and was, therefore, in the nature of a metaphorical statement of something on the earth not yet known or understood. Thus, the first two steps of the metaphorical process are already done for us. We start, then, at step three. We will write here some thoughts about stars in general and about this star in particular, and invite you to add as many items to the list as you can:

- the light of day comes from inside our solar system; the lights of night (except for the moon) from beyond it;

- a star is an extremely small light against an immense darkness;

- starlight requires darkness in order to be seen at all; it is easily overwhelmed by "brighter," that is, closer, lights;

- knowledge of the utter predictability of the stars was the earliest form of what we now would call scientific knowledge;

- this particular star is a maverick, belongs to no constellation, is like a comet, is a kind of lawbreaker;

- the order we see in the stars, e.g., the shape of the Big Dipper, is something of an illusion; if we could see the Dipper from the side instead of head on we would see that its stars are not on the same plane and are not really related to each other;

- the starlight we see is ancient; we see the stars as they used to be, not as they are now;

- we cannot see anything on earth by starlight;

- the darkness of night is transformed by the stars.

Add any other observations of your own:

Now, these points are made by taking the star image seriously for its own sake and not rushing to apply it metaphorically. Only after this has been done is it legitimate to transfer attributes from the metaphor to the original topic. The transfer, which Synectics calls "forced fit," proceeds in this manner: If, for example, the first attribute of the star is applied to Jesus it might mean that he belongs originally to a fundamentally different order from our own; the fifth might mean that somehow or other Jesus is a source of difference and surprise and is therefore a threat to ordinary stabilities; and so on. It is also possible, of course, that there may be no connection at all in any particular instance.

"Force fit" is the most important part of the metaphorical process because this is the step where the direct analogy is actually applied to the original question and made to yield up whatever new insight it may contain. Still, experience has shown that "force fit" can also be the most vexing part of the process. Synectics researchers have recently devised a simple but powerful way of doing the "force fit." They simply put the analogy into the form of an algebraic equation, and proceed to "solve for the unknown." In our present example, Jesus is being likened to a star, so that star = Jesus. But a more explicit and more practical version of this equation would be algebraic in form. Stated verbally, it would read: "This unique star is to stars in general as something unique about Jesus is to an ordinary personality." Or:

$$\frac{\text{Magi's star}}{\text{stars in general}} = \frac{\text{"x" about Jesus}}{\text{ordinary personality}}$$

"Force fitting," then, is the same thing as "solving for x." Some of the statements above about stars invite a comparison between Jesus and the Magi's unique star; to work with these statements, use the equation as written above. Other statements invite a comparison between any kind of star and Jesus; in these cases, use the following form of the equation:

$$\frac{\text{stars}}{\text{other sources of light}} = \frac{\text{"x" about Jesus}}{\text{other sources of divine knowledge}}$$

The Magi

We will repeat the process for the second part of the metaphor. We do this in order to get deeper into the text, and also to help you practice the third and fourth steps of the metaphorical process. Here, then, are some observations about the Magi, who journeyed by one kind of light in order to discover another:

● this kind of travel is possible only at night;

- the stars contain much more information about where we are located than the sun does;

- in this kind of travel the hands and feet—the "slower" senses—do the work that in daylight would be done by the eyes; that is, they tell us about our immediate surroundings;

- in this kind of travel the eyes are looking at the remotest possible things for help as one moves through the nearest possible things (the Magi have their eyes on the sky and their feet on the ground);

- our own solar system has to be darkened before the guiding lights show through;

- in this kind of travel the eyes work with the feet and hands more subtly than they do during day travel; the connection is much less direct;

- the Magi, unlike sailors, follow the maverick light, not the law-abiding ones;

- while accustomed to look for the ordinary and the predictable, the Magi were open to the extraordinary; surprise was as real to them as order.

Add any other observations of your own:

The Magi following the star somehow resemble people following Jesus. In formal terms, then, this idea would read: "The Magi in their relation to the star are as the followers of Jesus are to Jesus," or:

$$\frac{\text{Magi}}{\text{star}} = \frac{\text{"x" about Christians}}{\text{Jesus}}$$

As they used to say in algebra class, "Solve for x"!

When you finish doing this, you will have outlined a description of what a follower of Jesus is. Write out that description here.

In these two exercises you have had the opportunity to interpret someone else's direct analogies, but you were not able to create the analogies yourself. In the following brief exercise you may do exactly that, and in that way you will gain experience in working with steps one and two of the metaphorical process.

Think of some person who is especially important to you, for whatever reason. Write his or her name here:

To help you think through your feelings toward this person, find the most convincing answer to this question: What in the day or night sky *is* this person? Write as many answers as occur to you, then go back and pick the one that says it best. Name it here:

In the blank space write whatever you know about that object, regardless of whether any of its attributes seems to have any immediate connection with the person you are thinking about. Center your attention on the object, not the person.

Now is the time for the transfer. Allow each point you have made to be a *possible* point about the person you are thinking about. The less obvious connections will probably be the most provocative. Give yourself plenty of time to do this "force fit," and then take what you consider the most powerful of the metaphorical transfers and use them to complete this sentence:

This person is like

because

That, in its simplest essence, is how the metaphorical process works. The passage about the Magi illustrates how it works in a context outside the Hebrew Bible. Much of the rest of Matthew's gospel will show it at work within the Hebrew context. But it is always essentially the same process.

Matthew allows the Magi their page in his book, but not having any interest in the analogy between stars and humanity he makes certain their page is brief. He has another analogy he wishes to explore, in terms of which he has already defined his own existence and in terms of which he will try to define that of Jesus. Even before he gives the Magi their moment, he has already revealed the kind of metaphor that really interests him. In fact, the basic metaphor—Jesus = Old Testament—has already been announced three times before the Magi even appear. It takes the form of the three versions Matthew offers of Jesus' parentage.

Your Turn

We do not think as much in terms of pedigrees these days as people once did. To say one was a descendant of kings went a long way toward actually making one a king—and of thieves, a thief. There was not just hereditary wealth or poverty, as nowadays, but also what were thought to be inherited family traits which showed up, unchanged, as personal character traits. We might call this "source thinking." It is a way of thinking about someone, not in terms unique to the person but in terms of who (or what or where) he or she comes from. The person is thought of as derived rather than self-contained, and only by reference to something prior to him or her in both time and prestige is the person to be understood.

This exercise is designed to help you to do some "source thinking," in preparation for a discussion of Matthew's use of a similar process. Matthew was thinking about Jesus, who mattered enormously to him. Similarly, we ask you to name some person who matters greatly to you at this moment (perhaps the same person you named in the previous exercise) and to write that person's name at the base of the tree diagram, below.

Now, make a *metaphorical* family tree for this important person. We stress *metaphorical* because the point here is not to determine a literal record of generations. The point is to create an imaginary assembly of "ancestors" who, put together, suggest the character of this person. Fill in the items that ask what kind of sound, bird, plant would have been the "source" of this person.

Thinking Metaphorically about Someone Else

Test your analogies for their originality and aptness by asking someone else—perhaps the person they refer to—what he or she thinks you mean by each one. In general, direct analogies which are *not* immediately obvious stand a much better chance of being both more original and more thought-provoking than those which are too easily and too quickly understood.

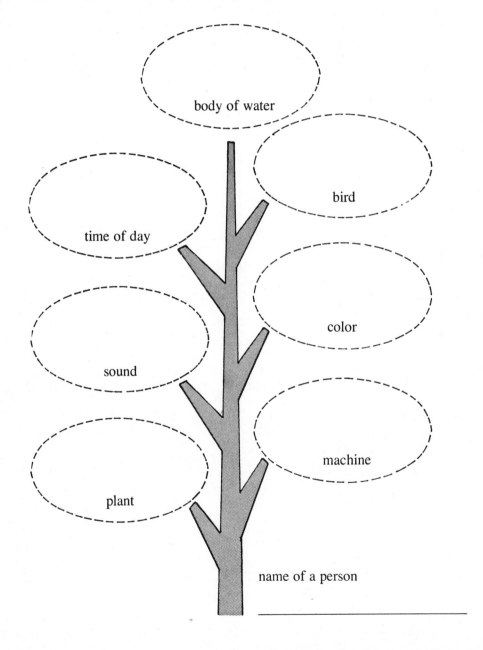

body of water

bird

time of day

color

sound

machine

plant

name of a person

_____

Thinking Metaphorically about One's Self

Now repeat the same process, using this tree to represent what *you* are like, something that metaphorically you are "descended" from.

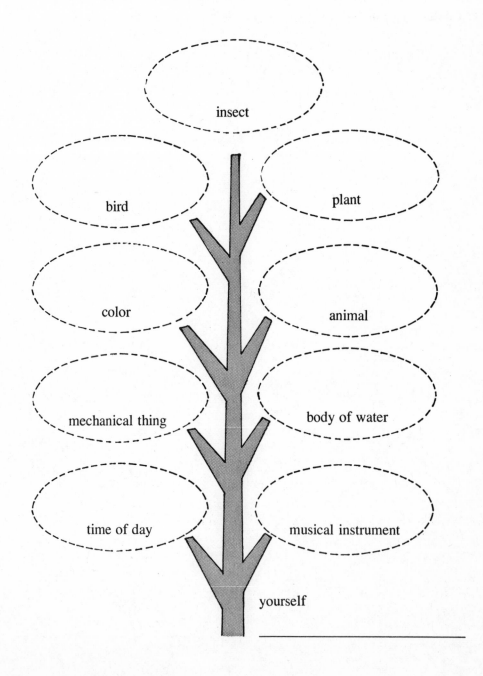

insect

bird

plant

color

animal

mechanical thing

body of water

time of day

musical instrument

yourself

_____

Are you clear in your own mind why you chose each metaphor for yourself? In the space available around each branch of the tree, jot down the specific connection you see between the analogy and yourself.

Are there aspects of each metaphor that do apply to you but that you didn't originally think of? Write them down in the margin.

Are there aspects of each metaphor that you emphatically feel do not apply to you? Write them down also. We urge you to write down all your answers because that will help you to be explicit.

If you would like to share this exercise with someone you know or care about, ask this person to fill out your genealogy from his or her own point of view, and then compare notes. Do the same for the other person's genealogy.

These two exercises on "source thinking" have been designed, chiefly, to show you how the metaphorical way of thinking can help you articulate your feelings about yourself and about other people. But they have also been designed to introduce you to the kind of thinking that made possible the construction of the three genealogies of Jesus to be found in the introductory chapters of Matthew's gospel.

Matthew's first and shortest genealogy calls Jesus "the son of David, the son of Abraham" (1:1). The second and longest counts down from Abraham through specific generations (1:2-16). The third (1:17) reduces the second list to three giant leaps: from Abraham to David, from David to the Babylonian Captivity, from the Captivity to Jesus. In each of these three versions of the genealogy Jesus is being compared to something different. The genealogies themselves are metaphorical. Their intention is to make a direct analogy between Jesus and something in the Hebrew past.

The shortest version equates Jesus to David and Abraham. David was the greatest Israelite king, who inaugurated an era of national pride and coherence—the golden age, in fact, of the Hebrew nation. Centuries before David, Abraham was the first person with whom God made his special covenant; he was the first person of religious faith as the Bible understands religion. As we shall see in greater detail below (see esp. Chapter 6), the ideas of covenant and kingdom as represented respectively by Abraham and David were virtually a summary of the Jewish religion. This first genealogy by Matthew therefore is a metaphorical statement to the effect that David–Abraham—who represent golden moments for the people of the biblical faith—express what we can expect from Jesus. Anyone familiar with the terms of the analogy, *David* and *Abraham*, would already know from the gospel's first sentence what Matthew thinks of Jesus.

Matthew's briefest genealogy makes one point about Jesus. But Matthew goes back and, as it were, asks himself whether he might not be able to make another point by using a metaphorical genealogy in some other way. He fills in the gaps between Jesus, David, and Abraham. But he fills them in quite selectively, with no eye to the accuracy demanded nowadays of the makers of family trees. These many fathers of Jesus are a kind of list of the characteristics of Israel, which are by metaphorical extension considered to be those of Jesus himself. Abraham, the man of faith; Isaac, the (almost) sacrificed son; Jacob, the father of the twelve sons from whom the twelve tribes will descend (as Jesus is the caller of the twelve from whom the Church would arise); and so on through a long list of much less well known figures from biblical history, each an exemplar of some aspect of the life of the Jewish people under God. To be compared to such a list is to be compared to the totality of the Hebrew experience. Matthew is making large claims for Jesus.

He makes a still bolder point in his third version of the metaphorical genealogies (1:17). He introduces a new analogy: numbers. The earlier lineage of Jesus breaks down into three sections of fourteen generations each. Fourteen is twice seven, and for the Jewish tradition seven was the number of the divine and of perfection. It is the number of the Sabbath day, which was at the heart of the normal piety of the nation. Jesus is *the* person of sevens, so to speak—the perfect, the divine, the center of religion. His coming will be as portentous an event for Israel as the coming of Abraham and David, and as uprooting as the exile to Babylon. His coming is the intervention of the divine.

Between Jesus and each of the three sets of analogies there is a different coherence. Matthew realizes that no one analogy can entirely say what Jesus is, that each can say only some part of what Jesus is like. All the direct analogies he uses so far were familiar parts of the Hebrew consciousness, and so Matthew is deftly telling his Jewish readers that they can readily understand Jesus in the terms of their inherited tradition.

That is, as we shall see, a very sensitive point within Christianity itself, one with which as notable a figure as John the Baptizer will take exception. There will be a quarrel within the gospel itself over the analogies which are here used to introduce Jesus. We will be witnesses of the attempt to find the right metaphors for Jesus, and witnesses of the way he will himself settle the problem.

In any case, Matthew's own basic position is clear—Jesus and the Old Testament are directly comparable. Or is that less clear than it at first seems? Closer examination shows that the comparison is not as direct and simple as it seems. It is, in fact, loaded with paradoxes and downright contradictions.

It is true that at every point Matthew is quick to quote from the Hebrew Bible something that analogizes even the infant Jesus to something from the past. The "virgin birth" means that he is Isaiah's "Emmanuel" (1:23). Being born in Bethlehem (2:6) equates him once again to David, who was also from there. Returning from Egypt (2:15) equates him to the Jewish nation in the Exodus. Again, his being born in Bethlehem connects him, in Matthew's view, with Rachel (2:18), because tradition placed her tomb near Bethlehem. So Matthew depicts Rachel as weeping for her own slaughtered children of old, for the slaughtered innocents of Bethlehem, and for Jesus himself, the innocent from Bethlehem who will be slaughtered on a distant tomorrow. All of this exemplifies Matthew's consistent use of relatively uncomplicated analogy.

But the very act of making direct analogies between Jesus and traditions of the Old Testament is paradoxical in itself. For many of the Jews will be presented in Matthew's own gospel as rejecting Jesus and he them. The antagonism between Jesus and the Hebrew tradition is at least as great as the harmony. Thus, if Matthew presents Jesus as the fulfillment of the Old Testament, he is also presenting him as its supplanter and saboteur. Clearly Matthew wants to stress the continuity so that Jewish people could more easily accept Jesus. But Jesus himself—as presented in Matthew's own gospel—stresses more and more the tension. If it is possible to be married and divorced at the same time, that is the relationship of Jesus and the Jews.

Matthew himself seems to be implicitly asserting the paradox within Jesus' relationship to the Jews. For his lengthiest genealogy (1:2-16), which thoroughly anchors Jesus to the totality of the Hebrew experience, ends with the figure of Joseph from whom *Jesus did not descend*. A conventional explanation of this oddity is that, although Matthew does not believe Joseph is Jesus' real father, still the line is traced through the putative father for reasons of legality and heredity. This may be so, but Matthew shows no signs of being interested mainly in legalities here. For example, he is perfectly willing to drop three known historical kings from his ancestral list (between Joram and Ozias in v. 8) for no other reason than to maintain the numerical symmetry of the three sets of fourteen generations. Clearly, he is constructing a genealogy more symbolic than literal, and it will have to be interpreted as a metaphor rather than as an historical or legal document. At the very least the genealogy suggests an ambiguity about Jesus' descent: he did *and he did not* descend from the Hebrew nation. He can *and he cannot* be understood in terms of the Hebrew experience.

But even if it is taken as a statement of what he did come from rather than of what he did not, the genealogy presents difficulties and embarrassments. Most of the kings mentioned in the list between David and the Babylonian Captivity are remembered as "bad" kings, and most of the people mentioned in the other lists are minor figures at best, thoroughly negligible people. Except for Abraham, David, and Solomon, Jesus' lineage is largely undistinguished, and the suggestion may be that to descend from the Hebrew nation is a very mixed thing consisting of three parts grandeur to roughly forty parts mediocrity. (The recipe, of course, is not a specialty of the Hebrews.)

But the real shock in the genealogy is to be found in the women. Legal genealogies traced only the male line. By including women Matthew stresses his indifference to the legalities and his commitment to symbolic statement. The women are Thamar (v. 3), Rahab (v. 5), Ruth (v. 5), Bathsheba the wife of Uriah (v. 6), and Mary herself (v. 16). Thamar was a prostitute (Gen. 28), Rahab was a prostitute (Jos. 2:1 and 6:23), Ruth was a pagan (see Book of Ruth), Bathsheba was an adulteress (2 Sam. 11ff.), and Mary was conspicuous mainly for her virginity. Jesus therefore comes from both promiscuity and virginity, and from both Jewry and paganism. If the genealogy makes Jesus the descendant and embodiment of the totality of the Hebrew experience, it is incredibly honest in presenting that experience for the highly ambiguous and compromised thing it really was. Insofar as Jesus descends from human antecedents, he comes from that which is most ordinary, which is to say both noble and sleazy. Jesus does not come from a romantic Israel nor from a lyrical humanity. He comes from the "unaccommodated thing itself," as King Lear called us all. If Matthew is making large claims for Jesus, he is making them most humbly indeed. For Matthew there is a doubleness about Jesus' relationship to the tradition, which itself has an unsettling doubleness about it. Jesus will not be easy to define.

Your Turn   And, indeed, none of us is easy to define. Doubleness and paradox are there in all of us. Go back for a moment to the metaphorical genealogy you created for yourself. Which *one* metaphorical ancestor do you have most in common with? Write it in the space below.

Don't bother listing what you have in common with it. Be more direct than that. If you could speak to that ancestor, what two questions above all others would you want to ask it, in order to gain an insight into its inner life? Write them here:

1.

2.

Now switch roles. In imagination put yourself in that ancestor's place. Become the ancestor. When you say "I" you should no longer mean the person you usually think you are. You should be saying "I" for the animal or color or machine, etc., from which you "descended." Get rid of your own point of view and enter into the other's.

Close your eyes a while and allow yourself to be the ancestor you have named.

Now, *as the ancestor*, answer the questions that you yourself have just posed. Write your answers here after thinking them through:

1.

2.

You have just done an exercise in personal analogy (see page 18 of the Introduction). In the context of this book we invite the reader to do personal analogy for two reasons, one psychological, one religious. The psychological value of personal analogy is that it helps one to break through the rigid structures of the "ego" and to try on a wider range of possible identities, thereby enriching one's inner life. The religious value is that it puts one more deeply in touch with one's fellow creatures through empathy and sympathy—an attitude of openness and participation essential to the religious way of life.

But it is often helpful to go another step in the exploration of a metaphor. This is the step called "compressed conflict" (see page 18 of the Introduction). Again, there are psychological and religious reasons for going through this kind of process. Psychologically, to look deliberately for paradox means to divest oneself of the narrow and conventional point of view; it means to have the courage of detaching oneself from egocentric habit and bias. Religiously, it means to reach for a higher and less obvious synthesis of the diversity of experience than can be achieved in more superficial ways of thinking.

We invite the reader, then, to reflect further on the personal analogy above with the help of compressed conflict. Search carefully through your personal analogy for *any two elements* (facts, ideas, feelings, actions) which are contradictory to each other in any way. List all of them you can find:

_____ vs. _____

_____ vs. _____

_____ vs. _____

_____ vs. _____

_____ vs. _____

_____ vs. _____

Look over all the words to find the two which seem to you to be in the boldest possible contradiction of each other. Make a two-word noun phrase out of them, in which the contradiction between them stands out strongly. (In later exercises when you are asked to compose a compressed conflict remember that it is usually best expressed as a two-word phrase, one word of which is a noun and the other an adjective modifying it. Such a phrase is commonly used by writers, especially by poets, as a highly condensed form of paradox.)

_____   _____
(adjective)   (noun)

There you have—or should have—a bull's-eye description of your metaphorical ancestor and, if you will look again, of yourself. For your ancestor was only a metaphor for *you*. In the space below explain how this compressed conflict phrase is a definition of you.

As we shall see presently, Matthew goes through a very similar process, and reduces the three genealogies of Jesus to one central paradox, or compressed conflict.

Matthew emphasizes the paradox in Jesus' lineage by his rather clear reference to what has come to be called the "virgin birth." Each of these two words has a complete meaning of its own which normally excludes the meaning of the other word. If there is a birth, there is not a virgin; if there is a virgin, there is not a birth. But in effect Matthew asserts to the contrary that the two words must be taken together if the nature of *this* birth is to be understood. He is as usual defining Jesus by metaphors, but now by the kind of conflicted metaphor that directly attacks normal ways of thinking. That kind of metaphor equates opposites, and thrives on a suspension of ordinary logic in a celebration of contradiction. This is not done out of perversity, but out of a conviction that "normal," rutted ways of thinking leave out too much of reality. Once again, for Matthew there is a doubleness about Jesus' birth that cannot be reduced to a neatly logical statement. Jesus is from here, and he is not from here. Both things together say what he is. Neither by itself can.

As though to emphasize the inadequacy of simple comparisons when it comes to understanding Jesus, Matthew surrounds the birth scene with further paradoxes. People from far away come to worship, while people from close by come for murder. There is a worshipped child. There are rich gifts in a context of total poverty. There is a cosmic plan of salvation endangered by human plots.

There are the brightness and the darkness—the star and the night. All these elements of paradox serve to highlight the uniqueness of the event, but they are more than theatrical effects. They are intended to lead to a more-than-conventional insight, that the life of Jesus will be lived at the point where the contradictions are the most intense. How could it be otherwise for someone who is at one and the same time from here and not from here—for someone who *is* a paradox, a union of opposites?

Your Turn
In the previous exercise you re-defined yourself in terms of a compressed conflict. Jesus has been defined paradoxically, too, in the phrase *virgin birth*. But the extraordinary power of the phrase to evoke a new way of thinking has been blunted by centuries of over-use, as well as by our modern rationalism which cannot see beyond the biological impossibility of the idea. Even so, the phrase itself—*virgin birth*—is too familiar. It is now a cliché, and its original power is probably not available to us. Still, the phrase fulfills all the requirements for a very powerful compressed conflict, and like all compressed conflicts contains a kind of universal quality, so that it can be applied to a number of other things which, at first sight, may seem to have nothing in common with each other.

Let us try to recapture the power of this great paradoxical phrase. Name a natural event which you have personally witnessed in the past week which can be metaphorically described as a virgin birth. (We are not thinking of any supposed spontaneous generation or combustion—take the two words in a *metaphorical* sense.) Name it:

Explain why the word *virgin* is appropriate and why the word *birth* is also:

Why can this event *not* be adequately described only as *virgin* or only as *birth*? Again write out your answer.

So the concept is at least a possible one, and not only possible but potentially quite powerful.

Now, to bring all this closer to home, name an experience of your own during the last two weeks that—again, metaphorically—can be called a virgin birth. (Never mind how trivial it may seem at first sight. If the phrase fits it, name it.)

Why is it *virgin*? Why is it *birth*? Write your answers.

Write down why it can *not* be adequately described only by *virgin* and only by *birth*.

The world is full of "virgin births," if only we choose to look for them. Matthew, of course, chose to look and found the most dramatic one.

Probably no one will ever improve on the phrase *virgin birth* as the supreme definition of Jesus and of those who identify themselves with him. Even so, each person will understand the phrase with a different personal nuance. This exercise has tried to help you to formulate your own insight into it.

There are two more paradoxes in these opening passages of Matthew's gospel that deserve attention. The first involves Herod, the second Matthew himself. There is the obvious conflict between Herod the King and the new child who is said to be destined to be a king. Nothing paradoxical there, just the predictable nervousness of those who sit on thrones. But in this context there is more than that at work. Kingship, as we shall see again later on, was a key idea for the Jewish people, but it was also one that was laden with much conflict. The *real* king of Israel was supposed to be God; David turned out to be an acceptable and great king because he saw himself as only a vice-regent of the real King. Herod, however, though king of the Jews, is the vice-regent of the Roman emperor, who is distinctly *not* God's vice-regent. If Jesus, too, is going to be the king of the Jews, he is automatically involved in the conflicts that would be inevitable whenever kingship is mentioned in a Jewish context. As king, is Jesus like Herod, like David, or like God? It is safe to say he will not be like Herod, however much Herod may fear it. The question, then, is: Is King Jesus like King David, or King God? The answer seems to be both. The genealogies put Jesus in David's line, while the prophecy quoted at his birth put him in God's. Is Jesus less than God by being equal to David, or equal to God by being greater than David? Again the answer seems to be yes to both, paradox notwithstanding.

Matthew—and everyone mentioned in Matthew's gospel, including Jesus himself—is engaged in the task of defining who Jesus is and what his existence means. To define Jesus' existence, Matthew and everyone else have to find what Jesus is most like and what he is most unlike, or, to change the words, what he blends into and what he stands out from. For *to exist* literally means *to stand out from* (Latin: *ex-stare*). One can "stand out from" something by being a projection or continuation of it; one can also "stand out from" something by resisting it or contrasting with it. In order to determine what it means to say that Jesus "ex-ists," it will be necessary to say what he "stands out from," both in the sense of comparison and in the sense of contrast.

Even in his first two chapters Matthew has given a hint of the complexity of the task. There is more to come. In the next chapter we will study how he and others define Jesus' basic way of "standing out." In the third and fourth chapters we will study the problems within Jesus' way of existing which unfold in the course of Matthew's narrative. In the following three chapters—again, following Matthew's narrative as it unfolds—we will study how Jesus himself tries to work out the contradictions inherent in his way of "standing out." And finally, in the closing chapter we will reflect on the transformation of that kind of existence into something new.

Father and Son:
Establishing the Metaphor

2. Jesus' Image
of God

(Matthew 3—4)

The Magi and their way of defining Jesus came and went in Matthew's gospel. They were temporarily interesting to the author. But the genealogies revealed the real focus of this document: the attempt to define Jesus' existence by comparisons and contrasts to the Old Testament, itself seen as an inconsistent and paradoxical standard. One unruly thing—the story of Jesus—is being measured against another unruly thing—the story of the Jews. That is true in Matthew's largely symbolic first two chapters which we have just considered; it is even truer in Matthew's next two chapters which we will consider now, and which give a fuller idea of how difficult it is to define the "existence" of Jesus. From what does he "stand out," whether to be identified with it or distinguished from it? In the idea of the Virgin Birth Matthew more than suggested that the work of defining Jesus would not be easy.

At first it appears that Jesus is being roughly equated with John the Baptizer. John's opening words to his audiences (3:2) and Jesus' opening words to his (4:17) are exactly the same: "Reform your lives! The kingdom of heaven is at hand." John protests his humility before Jesus (3:14), it is true, yet they both come on identically in calling the old order to task. The old order is represented by "the people," among whom the Pharisees and Sadducees are especially prominent; and both Jesus and John will succeed in making enemies of them. A first reading of these two chapters suggests that John and Jesus are in the same relationship to the Pharisees and Sadducees and, what is more, John's reaction to them (3:7ff) is very similar to that of Jesus to Satan himself (4:1ff), that is, a relationship of mutual rejection. Jesus, then, would be defining his mode of existence as John does—by pure negation. It would be as though he said, "This is what I am *not*."

But there is an uncomfortable logic here. If followed out, it would mean that the Pharisees whom both John and Jesus denounce and even "the people" whom they call to repentance would occupy the same position to them as Satan does to Jesus in the scene of the Temptations. The Jewish people therefore would be equivalently Satan! However much later traditions—some of them in the New Testament itself—may have savored the analogy, Matthew could not. He could not make the Jews diabolical because he is trying to portray Jesus himself as thoroughly a Jew, for the sake of converting the Jews. The comparison, then, between Jesus and John cannot be taken simply at face value.

We must begin to distinguish between Jesus and John. Clearly, then, both "stand out from" their coreligionists, but it is necessary to define further how they "stand out from" each other. A clue to the difference between them is that Jesus does not join John's bitter attack on the Patriarch Abraham (3:9-10): "Do not pride yourselves on the claim, 'Abraham is our father.' I tell you, God can raise up children to Abraham from these very stones. Even now the ax is laid to the root of the tree. Every tree that is not fruitful will be cut down and thrown into the fire." For John's hearers the patriarch is the essential source of their legitimacy before both the human race and God. He is *the* father of the faithful. John's talk of laying the ax to the root of the tree can, therefore, only be understood by his hearers as a metaphor of patricide, and of the ultimate kind of patricide that would kill not only the father of the body but also the father of the heart and of the soul.

John's attack on Abraham, then, seems gratuitous and even a little stupid. If John wants to return people to a right relationship with God, what better figure would he point to than that old man? Sterile, Abraham bore a son by God's power; once a father, he surrendered his son to God's demands. Abraham saw his own fatherhood as an accident of grace; he thought of Isaac not so much as his own son as, quite simply, one more part of God's universal and absolute dominion. And through it all Abraham was the father who had left his own fatherland in order to affirm God's fatherhood alone. What better story for a religious reformer in need of a text? What better model of the completely religious man? For Abraham himself would be the first to agree with John that God himself could raise up children from stones; indeed, for the purposes of raising up children, Abraham himself was a stone, and he knew it. He knew it was a credit to God and not to himself that Isaac ever came to be. If John ever met Abraham they would have had no arguments.

But John evidently thinks there is something perverse in the attachment the Pharisees feel for the Patriarch, and in their way of defining their own existence in terms of his fatherhood. John then challenges them with a paradox: God can raise up sons from stones! But that was always the point about Abraham as far as the Jews were concerned—through Abraham, God *did* raise up sons from a stone. John's vehement challenge is therefore pointless, for what he offers as a triumphant rebuttal is the very thing his audience has assumed all along about their descent from Abraham.

Jesus does not get involved in this odd tangle. Indeed, he does something very similar to what the Pharisees do; namely, in his baptism he is defined as his father's son. He affirms something close to what the Pharisees affirm, the paternity of heaven and the sonship of the earth. There is, as we shall see, a crucial difference between these two *affirmations* of fatherhood and sonship. John, on the other hand, affirms nothing. He merely denies the value of Abraham's fatherhood. And as an inevitable consequence he denies the value of the centuries of fidelity and infidelity, of hope and of test, lived by the Jews under the mantle of the Patriarch. John is purely the negator. For the Pharisees, to exist at all means to "stand out from" the father; but John, denying them their father, therefore denies them existence itself.

The only figure equivalent to John in the passages under consideration is that of Satan in the scene of Jesus' temptations. Indeed, *the* temptation of Jesus is to deny that his true source is in his father and not in himself. John and Satan do a similar thing when they ask that humans stop defining themselves in terms of the sources from which they spring. Jesus does not join either of them in the denial. Satan he rejects out of hand. John—who, after all, is not a devil and who is passionately if erratically interested in restoring the purity of religion—will be simply deflated later on in the gospel with a beautifully ironical compliment: "I solemnly assure you, history has not known a man born of woman greater than John the Baptizer. Yet the least born into the Kingdom of God is greater than he" (11:11). From John's kind of vision nothing can come. He denies what has been fertile and is left waiting in his beloved desert for the stones to bring forth children for God.

But if Jesus "stands out from" the Baptist, he does not therefore blend into the Pharisees. Their affirmation and his are not the same. The great moment in which his special way of existing is defined is his baptism. John's baptism was a "baptism of repentance," typically, an affair of denials and rejections; but in Jesus' case it was more than that. It was the moment in which was revealed that from which Jesus "stood out," that in terms of which he existed. What John denied, God affirmed: paternity and sonship. For Jesus these were to be the terms in which all his life would be lived. Indeed, there would be no plot nor project to his life except to explore what is meant by those two words. Here was the central relationship that would give a structure to life and a purpose to action. Jesus stands out from God, but from God defined specifically as father.

The Pharisees saw themselves similarly. But the great difference is that their God-derived existence came through the medium of Abraham and his generations, while between Jesus and his ultimate father there is no intermediary. The moment of baptism is the moment in which the medium is cancelled for Jesus and the relationship of father and son is made immediate and simple.

The Magi had their star, Matthew his Bible, the Pharisees their Patriarch, through which to surmise the divine. Jesus has none of them. He has his father direct.

Or rather, there *is* a medium through which he relates to God. It is the medium of the word *father* itself. The word is a metaphor, taken out of its primary meaning of sexual parentage and human family life. There are some dimensions of the word—such as these just mentioned—which are clearly inappropriate as attributes of God. There are other dimensions of the word which are at best problematic when applied to God—for instance, that fathers and sons are notorious for struggling with each other at least as much as for reflecting each other. In the baptism Jesus has his God direct—or, better, almost direct. There is still a glass he has to look through, the metaphor of father and son.

The difference with the Pharisees is in the nature of the medium or context of the relationship with God. The relationship for them depends on a biological and cultural tradition; accordingly, to sustain the relationship with God it becomes supremely important to sustain the cultural legacies, the ethnic ways of doing things, the laws sanctioned by long tradition, the inherited mannerisms and attitudes—the whole art of belonging to a particular spot in space and a particular current of time. But if one's God is immediately one's father, all of that ceases to be actively important.

Jesus is more like John than like Satan, and more like the Pharisees than like John. But he is not really like them, either. By juxtaposing all these figures, Matthew has made it clear that Jesus has his own way of existing. He stands out alone, from God alone. The purpose of his gospel, and of our study of his gospel, is to explore the implications of that kind of existence.

The scenes of the baptism and the temptations show rather neatly the main problem of that kind of existence. In the baptism Jesus is defined purely in terms of the source from which he comes. But in the temptations he is asked to define himself as his own source. Jesus is confronted by Satan with the fact that he himself is powerful, can make decisions, work wonders, plan his own future, provide for his own needs, protect himself from dangers—in short, he can do for himself what we expect of any mature, self-reliant adult. He can be, as we say, his own person. Satan confronts Jesus, not only with tricks or evil possibilities, but with a positive and valid ambition. He is reminding Jesus the he is—or can be—his own source and center. But what for most people is their basic aspiration would be for Jesus the deepest betrayal. This is the one thing that can destroy the baptismal metaphor he has just founded his life upon. All fatherhood, all sourcehood, all initiatives, all plans, all decisions are God's because God is the universal and absolute father. Jesus does not define himself as the self-reliant man but as the father-oriented son. Satan, who is the voice not so much of evil as of common sense, speaks for the program of life which cannot belong to one who is above all else the son of his father.

It would seem, then, that in the temptations Jesus adopts a viewpoint similar to John the Baptizer's, and simply rejects any other source than God as simply an affront to God. But the whole matter is more complicated than that. Satan's temptations, though they are indeed temptations toward an affirmation of self in a denial of God, are much more specific than that. They are temptations to particular kinds of self-affirmation, not to some generalized sort. Each of the three temptations presents Jesus with a highly particular way of defining himself, and in rejecting each in turn it is not completely clear whether he is rejecting *just these ways* of asserting his own independent being, or rejecting *any kind* of independent existence as such.

For Satan, as usual, is subtle. It had been his business in the Old Testament to tease God into awareness of certain problems he otherwise would have overlooked. For example, in the Book of Job Satan taunted God with the idea that the experience of unmerited suffering would turn people away from faith and piety and that, by implication, God would do well to be kinder to his faithful. Here he taunts Jesus with the similar result of making him face a problem about himself. Jesus has just experienced what it is to be totally the God-centered, father-derived man. Satan presents him with three ways of being God-centered which are thoroughly sanctioned by the Old Testament. He proposes that Jesus try them on for size. He is offering Jesus the Old Testament itself as a model for defining himself—Satan as Pharisee! (And Satan as Matthew?)

The first temptation is to turn stones to bread (4:3). This is a coded way of saying: Do what Moses did in the desert for his people during the Exodus. Be Moses. (And is not Jesus, according to Matthew, to be the new Moses?)

The second temptation is to expect the care of angels wherever he goes, whatever he does (4:6). This is a coded way of saying: Be the Messiah, the anointed of God to whom, as it says in Psalm 91 which Satan quotes here, God has given all power and on whom he has lavished all his care and to whom he has, as it were, loaned his angels. (And is not Jesus, according to Matthew, to be the "messiah," which is Hebrew for *the anointed one,* which in its Greek form is the word *Christ?*)

The third temptation is to be king of a world united under his sole rule (4:9). This is a coded way of saying: Be King David. (And is not Jesus, according to Matthew, to be the "king," or, as Matthew has called him in the gospel's first verse, "Jesus Christ, Son of David"?)

It is difficult at first sight to see anything at all in these temptations which does not correspond exactly to one of the main ambitions of the New Testament in general and of Matthew in particular, namely, to identify Jesus as the continuation and perfection of the personages, institutions, and symbols of the Hebrew Bible. Jesus himself will repeat often that his vocation is precisely this (e.g., see 5:17). In the Sermon on the Mount he will deliberately appear in the guise of a new Moses, lawgiver on the mountain top; in his increasing exercise of divine power he will deliberately provoke a comparison of himself to the Messiah; and in his triumphant entry into Jerusalem (21:4ff) he uses what must be called conscious theatrical effects—the ass and foal to allude to kingly passages from Isaiah and Zechariah—to evoke the memory of David, and of the golden age of the kingdom. Jesus, then, does yield to Satan's temptations, and yields luxuriously. Indeed, he even yields to the second one the very moment Satan has vanished, for as soon as Satan is gone Jesus accepts what he had rejected a moment before: the care of angels (4:11). Clearly Jesus yields repeatedly to the temptations, but not when Satan proposes them.

His rejection of Moses, Messiah, and David is therefore quite unlike John's rejection of Abraham. Jesus' rejections are neither qualified nor absolute. Both Jesus and Satan are more subtle than John, making more distinctions than he, searching out more devious questions than he ever thought of. John is a great simplifier and over-simplifier. But Jesus and his tempter have a taste for the niceties of a question, for it is on the subtler points, not on the gross ones, that arguments are mainly won or lost.

The real temptation is not whether Jesus will try on being Moses or Messiah or David. Those are surface issues here, three disguised versions of the one real temptation. Satan is himself the real temptation. What is being proposed is that Jesus adopt Satan's way of being, rather than "standing out from" God as son from father, that is, as the father's continuation, his emanation, his *like.* In the temptations Satan "stands out from" God as his challenger, his irritant, his opposition, his *unlike.* One is an existence by comparison, the other by contrast, with the father.

God may look at Moses and see a God-centered man, or at the Messiah or David and see the same thing, but Satan looks at them and sees something different. He does not see men who are submissive but men who are powerful; he does not see humility but power; he does not see faith—once more he sees power; he does not see adoration and surrender—again he sees power: power to make bread of stones, power to assert oneself in the teeth of dangers, power to lord it over a universe of adoring subjects. He sees in human beings the potential to enjoy in their own right the same sovereignty, the same self-sufficiency, the same splendor which God enjoys in his. Satan, in effect, proposes that the distinction between God and humanity is an artificial one, held in place by force, fear, and illusion. It can be done away with.

Jesus' choice, then, would appear to be either acceptance of John's purely God-centered way of being or acceptance of Satan's purely self-centered way of being. We have already seen that, though he is indeed God-centered, Jesus does not go with John in his denial of other kinds of centers of existence, specifically the patriarch Abraham. It begins to seem, too, that Jesus' rejection of the tempter's self-contained kind of existence is less than complete, for with no hesitation he will take as his own the divine prerogatives of power and glory. Here, then, is Jesus' decision about how to "ex-ist": neither John's way nor Satan's, but both. Each of them has a hand on the truth, but the left and right hands refuse to acknowledge each other's part of the truth. Jesus then will exist from the Father purely, as the baptism establishes; but that existence will be an affair of both John and Satan, of comparisons and contrasts, continuities and discontinuities, submission and assertion, sameness and change—in a word, it will be an affair of paradox.

Your Turn   From one point of view Jesus is unique, and his baptism and temptations are unique. But Christianity has always stressed, in addition to his quality of unrepeatable uniqueness, his universality. He may be the only one of his kind, but he is also understood as the pattern or archetype of us all. If that is so, his unique baptism and temptations must in some way be reflected or approximated in the experience of everyone.

In the genealogy exercises of the last chapter you were introduced to what we called "source thinking." We suggested that this was the kind of thinking Matthew did about Jesus in constructing his genealogies. But now it becomes clear that it is the kind of thinking Jesus himself is doing, as he defines himself in terms of the ultimate source from which he comes and toward which he goes. Indeed, Jesus thinks in terms of a source more ultimate than Matthew explicitly names, and in effect writes for himself the briefest genealogy of all: "Jesus Christ, Son of God." The lesser, secondary sources all vanish in this affirmation of the highest one, as stars disappear in the light of the sun.

We asked you to construct a metaphorical pedigree for yourself. But now construct a literal one. Name at least twenty less-than-ultimate sources—twenty sources this side of God, that is—from which you derive your existence. These sources may be biological (such as your genes), chemical (such as the oxygen you breathe), cultural (such as your nationality).

The range is very large, for we come from many sources. Write twenty of your sources in the space available below.

Did you name any one source in your list from which you feel the whole of your existence is derived? If so, which one? and why?

If you did not name such a source (and the instructions for the exercise asked you *not* to!), try to do so now. What would you regard as your *ultimate* source, the source of all the other sources? Write its name.

Jesus called his ultimate source *father*, since he experienced it as calling him *son*. These are words which attempt to describe the indescribable. The history of Christianity—and one of the main tasks of this book—has been to understand the meaning of those words.

But there is a problem with those words. We can look at *father* or *son* as referring to a very wide range of experience. If used by themselves without reference to a particular relationship, they are almost too general to mean anything. If used to refer to any one particular father-son relationship, they tend to become too unique to mean anything else. Besides, as we shall see later in this book, the words can be disturbingly ambiguous.

We would like in the following exercise for you to do some "source thinking"—without, however, having to encounter the difficulties hidden in those seemingly innocent words, *father* and *son*. Since *father* is itself a metaphorical way of defining what the ultimate source is, we will simply replace that metaphor with another; we will do the same with the word *son*. Among other things, both words are exclusively masculine. God of course is neither male nor female. It would be helpful here to choose a metaphor for one's "source" that simply sidesteps the problem of attributing a sex to God.

What in the world of nature has an ultimate source from which it comes and to which it returns? We would like to suggest an answer to that question: the Pacific Northwest salmon, whose source is the pool in which it is born, from which it migrates and to which it returns to spawn and die. The pool is a very real kind of ultimate source, and it exerts a profound influence on the salmon's entire life cycle.

The principal metaphorical process you will use in the following exercise is personal analogy. You will "be" the salmon. It will be important to identify fully with the salmon as it goes through its cycle of changing relationships to its source. In each of the steps in the exercise, allow the experience of the salmon to become your own. To help your imagination, allow yourself to identify with a particular salmon, that is, give it some particular qualities of size, speed, color.

The exercise is in five stages. Read through the instructions for each stage, then set aside the text, close your eyes, and recreate the scene in your imagination. Feel yourself reliving the salmon's experience from within. When you feel you have finished doing this, write out your experience as the salmon in the space available. *Write always in the first person*. When you have finished this, go on to the next stage and repeat the process.

Stage One

Life begins for you in a quiet river bed. There are many hundreds of others like you, very small, full of energy. There are many others much larger, much slower, some of them not moving at all except as the currents move them. There are green leaves and roots, living but not moving on their own. The rocks and stream bed soon become familiar, almost a part of you. The smells are what you notice most. You become familiar with each smell of this place. You can find your way about by the odors. They become your guide. You spend your days finding food. As you grow and forage, the pond becomes more and more a part of you.

Stage Two

Many months have passed and something inside you says it is time to leave this place. You have matured. This pond is no longer enough, and so you, and the others, begin to move with the current. Your pond, so long familiar, will still be with you, especially the familiar odors of the green living things and the rocks which have been your guides for food and protection. As the current begins to carry you along and ease your journey downstream you pick up new, unfamiliar odors. Each new smell becomes a part of you. You record it all. You find yourself moving faster, over rock, down waterfalls, and then you find yourself in a wider, deeper water, moving more slowly in a vaster world. Something is changing.

Stage Three

The water is deeper, far beyond anything you have known. The currents have changed drastically. There are infinitely more life forms than you have ever seen. Above all, the water itself is different, and you have to make the change from fresh water to salt. But some things remain familiar. You remain with the others, though there are not so many of you now. Your sense of smell still helps you to find food, but the many new and changing smells can no longer be guides for a journey.

Stage Four

You grow as months and months pass. Something inside of you begins to feel complete. Your body, which has been growing and changing, is now strong and seems finished; and once again something in you and the others says it is time to leave. Now you know there is something you must do that you can do only where you began your life. You must find the river. Your guide has something to do with the light in the water—not the smells.

Stage Five

You find your way with the others back to the river, and as soon as you arrive the water changes back to its old familiar feeling and smell. As soon as you begin to follow the smells which you remember, something becomes more difficult. You have to struggle against the water and up the rocks. You are cut, bruised, and battered. But you must return, and the smells continue to guide your journey. Days of constant struggle begin to sap your strength, but you are coming closer to your pond. The smells become more and more familiar until you are back to the very first scents you can remember. Back at this place now, you are able to pass on the life you have received. You have enough strength for that alone. With the last bit of strength you have, the life passes out of you to begin its course again in others who do not yet know where it will take them.

If you have been able to identify with the salmon, you have experienced something like the kind of "source thinking" which Jesus did.

Reflect a bit further on the experience. What part of the salmon's cycle is most like the present stage of your life? Explain why.

Do you in your normal consciousness of things think of yourself:

a. strictly in terms of the here and now;
b. primarily in terms of your fairly immediate personal sources; or,
c. primarily in terms of your ultimate source?

Identify which is the most characteristic of you.

If you were to begin thinking in one of the other two, less characteristic ways about yourself, what would change in your values, feelings, behaviors, relationships?

What is lost by defining yourself *only* in terms of your proximate but still secondary sources, to the exclusion of thinking of yourself as having an ultimate source? (Remember that this is very much like what the Pharisees tended to do.)

On the other hand, what is lost by thinking of yourself *only* as derived from an ultimate source, to the exclusion of everything else? (Remember that this is like what John the Baptizer asked everyone to do.)

Again, what is lost by thinking *only* in the here and now, by thinking of oneself as one's own sufficient source to the exclusion of everything else? (This, of course, is what Satan asked Jesus to do.)

"Source thinking," as Jesus knew and as perhaps now you have found out, can free us to think of ourselves in new, sometimes profoundly new, ways. It helps us to identify that from which or against which we "stand out." And remember that to "stand out" means to "exist."

In the two chapters under consideration here, Matthew has tried to help us define who Jesus is and what his way of being is by juxtaposing him to the figures of John, the Pharisees, and Satan. In each case there is a major point of comparison and a major point of contrast, and the cumulative effect is a dawning realization in the reader of the richness and uniqueness of this figure whose book Matthew has undertaken to write.

Jesus is like John in his radical affirmation of the primacy of God. God is the sole source, universal father. Jesus is unlike John, however, for he does not hold that the paternity of Abraham—and consequently of the whole Old Testament tradition which flows from it—is in competition with the paternity of God. Not all other fatherhoods defy God's; some might even embody it and participate in it.

Jesus is like the Pharisees, then, in affirming the Old Testament. He is unlike them, however, in not attributing intrinsic importance to the particular cultural milieu in which the fatherhood of God is there celebrated. Though he certainly does not reject Abraham as John does, he is a lot looser about Abraham than the Pharisees are. God is father both through Abraham and altogether apart from him. God is both present in and free from the people and traditions of Israel.

Jesus then is like John and unlike the Pharisees and Satan in rejecting the temptation to identify himself with figures from the Old Testament, especially if that is somehow to deny the primacy of God. But he is like Satan, too, in implicitly realizing the possibility of a personal source that is neither God nor the Old Testament but oneself, pure and simple.

Jesus is to be the son of the father, and in his third and fourth chapters Matthew has already given us a sense of how unprecedented that sonship will be. It will be a sonship made of elements of John, Pharisee, and Satan—and a sonship that will deny elements of all three. An affair, again, of paradox.

In our own third and fourth chapters below we will study Jesus' earliest experiences in living out his life under the terms of the metaphor of father and son. We will see the life of increasing conflict he has to live—conflict without and conflict within—because of that very metaphor. In Chapters 5, 6, and 7 we will reflect on three different ways in which Jesus experiences the paradoxical nature of his way of being. By the end of the temptations, all three paradoxes are latent, but Jesus will have to live out each of them explicitly before the end can come. Briefly, the three paradoxes are these:

First, does the metaphor of father and son have a *liberating or a confining effect* on the one who lives in its terms? That is, is it liberating, a source of pride and power, a thing of growth and freedom—in other words, does it enhance humanity as Satan would enhance it; or, to the contrary, is it constrictive and reductive, a source of humiliation, a cause of paralysis, a source of self-annihilation—that is, does it put humanity in its place before the power of God, as John would do? Jesus will have to experience both possibilities before he is through. This first paradox will be more fully explored in Chapter 5.

Secondly, does the metaphor of father and son have *a collective, or an individual, sanction*? That is, does its authority come from Hebrew tradition as the Pharisees would have it, or from one's subjective experience as Satan would have it? And how do these two kinds of authority interact? Once again, Jesus will have to experience both ends of the paradox before he is through. The second paradox will be explored in Chapter 6.

Thirdly, metaphor itself is paradoxical—both *an image* of reality *and a distortion* of it, or, perhaps more accurately, a limited and limiting way of seeing it. The most serious of all the paradoxes Jesus will have to deal with is this: Is his metaphor more successful as an expression of the reality of God—as the Pharisees believe of their metaphors? Or is it more of a distortion or limitation of that reality—as John believes about the metaphors of old? Again, Jesus will have to experience both possibilities to the full. This third paradox will be the subject of Chapter 7.

But before we can deal with these three paradoxes we must look at how Jesus begins his new life as the son of this father. The temptations over and the baptismal metaphor confirmed, Jesus' first act is to call others to join him (4:18ff). To do so they must leave their nets and their boats, as Jesus before them has left behind the ambition of self-reliance, financial prudence, ordinary humanity. But even that is not enough. In order to follow Jesus they must leave behind something deeper than their tools and their livelihood. They must abandon *their fathers*. There are no more fathers but one, for the God-afflicted person. All other centers collapse into that one center, like the matter of a collapsing star. Abraham and all the fathers disappear into God. They may re-emerge, transformed. But at first they must simply disappear. If *the* father is to be affirmed, the many fathers must, for at least a while, be denied.

The metaphor is chosen. Like all significant metaphors, it epitomizes and expresses a past experience and implies a course of future actions. But, even though the future is somehow contained in it, still that future has to be discovered by one's living out the metaphor day in and day out. The future is not contained in the metaphor as beans are contained in a can, but as a plant is contained in a seed. Choosing a metaphor by which to define one's life does not mean taking uncertainty out of the future, for one does not know at the beginning all the secrets that have been folded up in the metaphor. Therein lies for all people the high drama which Jesus' baptism and temptations exemplify. For at this moment of illumination, of brilliant insight into God and into his own relationship with God, Jesus does not know and has no clue to suggest that living out the poetry of this exquisite metaphor will lead to the cross. Jesus has already chosen his future, but does not yet know what it is.

Father and Son:
Establishing the Metaphor

3. The Image of God as Guide

(Matthew 5:1–16)

In the last chapter we explored the definitive and defining act of Jesus' life. It was the act of establishing the right metaphorical terms by which to express his fundamental experience and to project the values and attitudes upon which he would act. He experiences God as father, experiences himself as son. The single metaphor will operate as the unifying and simplifying point of view from which Jesus will see all things.

But metaphors, even grand ones such as this, seem harmless enough. Literarily graceful, aesthetically satisfying, they can easily seem not to be doing much work of any importance. And that may be true for those metaphors which decorate language rather than stimulate thought. But there are other metaphors which are designed for heavy-duty work, and indeed some of them are designed to do the heaviest work of all, that of establishing a world view. Such working metaphors inevitably imply paradoxes that unsettle the established ways of seeing things. When, for example, in the late 17th and 18th centuries people began to think of the world as a huge clock, the consequence of the metaphor was a paradox. As a clock the world was both more intelligible (and therefore more comfortable) for human beings to live in and also more impersonal (and therefore less comfortable) for them to live in. The one metaphor had two equal but opposite effects. Indeed, only when a great metaphor has been stripped down to its central paradox can it really be said to be understood.

If metaphor is the making equal of things not equal, paradox is the making equal of things directly opposite and totally unequal. By paradox one sees unity not only in things that are similar but in things that are contradictory. The power of a great metaphor lies in its ability to push the mind to the end of logic, and there, at the brink of chaos, to consider something new.

And it is almost always at the brink of chaos that new insight comes. The clock metaphor mentioned above replaced the medieval metaphor of hierarchy. The world was no longer a layered series of personal beings leading upward to God; it was a whirling series of wheels and gears going around forever almost but not quite in circles. In between the two metaphors there was a time of chaos: "'Tis all in pieces," said John Donne during that time, "all coherence gone." The new metaphor replaced both the old metaphor and the chaos that resulted from its collapse. But at the same time it paradoxically opened up a new disorder, in the case of this example the disquieting idea that a human being is utterly isolated in a world at once intelligible and cold. At the heart of a powerful metaphor is paradox.

If religious language is intrinsically metaphorical, it therefore must also be intrinsically paradoxical. The power of a new religious metaphor such as Jesus' lies in the paradoxes it contains. Indeed, the paradox *is* the new idea. It is the source of new ways of being.

Your Turn   Before examining the Beatitudes themselves, which are the topic of this chapter, we should test the idea that the paradox or compressed conflict phrase which best defines the kind of person you are also defines the kind of attitudes and energies you bring to any situation.

Go back a moment to the personal analogy exercise you did on the salmon. Go back specifically to the section of the exercise you identified as most resembling your present life (never mind if the resemblance is not perfect). Re-read the notes you made on your fantasy experience there, looking for any elements that seem in tension with each other or are even contradictory to each other. Experiment with several possible combinations until you have come up with the compressed conflict phrase that most perfectly captures the inner dynamism of that experience.

As the first step in this exercise, write that compressed conflict phrase in the box at the center of the figure below. The innermost circle will stand for you.

As Jesus' relationship to his ultimate source was tested in his conflict with Satan, so the same relationship would be his guide in his dealings with the world. He would find an increasing series of conflicts with that world as he sought to live and work in it and to keep alive the awareness of his relationship to his father.

This exercise is designed to explore what happens when someone tries to keep alive that sense of relatedness to an ultimate source and to act coherently with it amid the various tensions in the world.

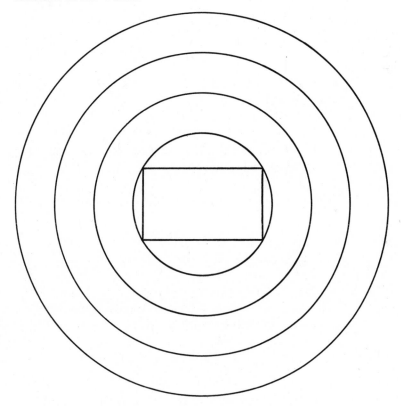

The circles other than the innermost one represent the several "worlds" through which you move. To take the second step in this exercise, write in each circle, what you call that "world." Be specific. Call it "Smith's Grocery," not just "where I work"; or "P.S. 122," not just "school."

The third step, of course, will be to relate the compressed conflict phrase in the center to those other worlds. Before doing that with a real-life situation, though, try it on a fictitious one. Here is a problem anyone might encounter in one of his or her "worlds":

"I happen to have some extra money for a change. Do I spend it on my children—who are not over-privileged or spoiled—or do I donate it to a very worthy cause?"

There is a moral dilemma. Suppose for the sake of the exercise that the compressed conflict that defined your essential character had been something like "A Violent Calm." If you were a "violent calm," how would you resolve the moral dilemma? and why?

Again for practice, repeat the exercise, using the compressed conflict "benign neglect" as the definition of your central character.

Do it once more, but use the actual compressed conflict you placed in the center of the circle of the figure above.

In each case there was a tension of opposing values and attitudes, and the business of deciding how to act in a specific case involved finding the most satisfying and convincing balance of those tensions. It seldom if ever means just getting rid of one side of the tension in favor of the other.

Now repeat the entire exercise, this time "for real." Identify which of the four "worlds" you named is in the area of a genuine moral dilemma that you presently face. Describe exactly what that moral dilemma is.

How would a person defined by the compressed conflict written in the center circle handle this problem?

As we shall see presently, Jesus too reduced his own life, and that of everyone who wished to be thought of as a child of the Father, to a key paradox. He expressed that paradox in the sublime opening words of the Sermon on the Mount. And in the paradoxes he expressed there, he announced the essence of a whole new way of living and acting in the world.

This chapter is devoted to a consideration of the brief passage called the Beatitudes (5:1-16). The reason for giving attention to so small a text is not that the text is one of extraordinary poetic beauty, although that alone would justify our lingering over it. The reason is rather that this, the first significant public statement of Jesus in Matthew's gospel, this meticulously worded inaugural address, contains nothing but paradoxes. In addition to introducing his message for the first time, Jesus is also proclaiming that the essential feature of his way of thinking is to turn everything upside down and inside out.

Each of the Beatitudes contains two sentences connected by the explanatory conjunction "for." The second part gives the reason for the blessedness of the people mentioned in the first. The form of the Beatitudes, then, is virtually that of a logical syllogism—logical in form, illogical in content:

If one inherits the earth, then one is blessed.

But the meek will inherit the earth.

Therefore blessed are the meek.

It is precisely because they are presented as being perfectly logical that the Beatitudes are so irritating, for a breach of common sense is being disguised as rational. Something is asserted as necessarily true which nothing in ordinary experience will confirm.

What Jesus has done can be clarified if we more closely examine the Beatitudes in their syllogistic form. The third term follows correctly from the first two. The first term is a matter of conventional wisdom. Jesus agrees with it, his hearers agree with it, the whole Jewish tradition emphatically agrees with it. Inheriting the earth, having a first and firm claim on their own territory, had been one of the overriding preoccupations and one of the most frustrating ambitions of the Jews for centuries. The same consensus existed for the first term of each of the Beatitudes. To own the kingdom of heaven, to be comforted, to inherit the earth, to have one's hunger and thirst satisfied, to obtain mercy, to be on intimate terms with God, to be known even as the children of God—this is virtually a list of the classical ambitions of the Hebrew people. It is also a list of what never quite happened to them. It is, then, an especially poignant grouping of things, the things everyone wants and no one has, the common hope and the common humiliation. Jesus is addressing himself squarely to the traditional values of his people. And everyone accepts the first term of each of his implied syllogisms. It would be good to have these things come true.

The outrage lies in the second term, which in each case is not only different from the received idea but is in direct contradiction to it. Being poor in spirit, having altogether too much reason to mourn, being meek, hungry, and thirsty, taking no revenge because too feeble to reinforce it, being simple because unable to be otherwise, always calling for peace because unable to win a war—these were experienced universally in the Jewish tradition as the ingredients of an almost daily misery. In the second term of each of his implied syllogisms Jesus asserts the paradox that the ingredients of misery are the ingredients of happiness. He stops the conventional wisdom dead and says that, in what they dread, the people will find what they want. It makes as much sense as to say Abraham's fatherhood is in opposition to God's, or to say that Jesus both is and is not descended from Abraham, which is to say that it makes no immediate sense at all.

Is there, perhaps, something merely perverse in this taste for paradox? The desire to shock or to stand things on their head can be strong enough to be its own motive. When Oscar Wilde said that something was "as beautiful as the seven deadly sins," he was indulging a taste for paradox too. Is Wilde to be taken as seriously as Jesus—or, for that matter, is Jesus to be taken as lightly as Wilde? It seems clear that most of Wilde's little ironies are meant mainly for laughter and only slightly for further thought, while Jesus' paradoxes do not amuse at all but stir up either serious thought or serious anger. What makes the difference?

There is no doubt more than one answer to that question, but a good deal of the answer lies in the investigation of a further question: What is the motive behind the paradox? A paradox can come either from the desire simply to negate the conventional wisdom, or from the desire to affirm an alternative one. It is not always easy to tell the difference between the two. For example, when van Gogh painted the starry night not as a thing of quiet beauty but as a mass of swirling suns spinning off currents of almost terrifying power, many people responded to the paradox as merely insane—a defiance of the ordinary viewpoint, not the advent of a new and somehow deeper one. But for van Gogh the world was a system in turmoil with itself, just as he was in turmoil with himself. Everything became a metaphor of that central energy which, like fire, made things bright to make them beautiful, but which also, again like fire, made them bright only to burn them out. Van Gogh did not set out to outrage the conventional way of seeing; he set out rather to announce his own special way of seeing, an alternative way, and inevitably wound up producing paradoxes. He created a metaphor different from everyone else's, a different paradigm of reality.

The kind of irony that merely negates the conventional wisdom is tied to that wisdom. The conventional view is, so to speak, its hidden agenda. It has no soul of its own. It exists as a reaction only. It has a value—that of teasing us, of making us take ourselves more lightly—but it does not lead to a new idea, nor, for that matter, does it really test the value of the old.

It should be clear now what Jesus has done in the Beatitudes. He has worked off of the old idea, but not merely out of a taste for contradicting it. Rather, he is bringing the old idea into contact with his own new idea. His new idea is contained in the metaphor that God and God alone is the father, and that he is father both within and without the terms of the Hebrew tradition. In the Beatitudes Jesus begins to spell out what is involved in being a son to that father. In the old view the world was seen as primarily a power structure, with God (or God and King) on top dispensing judgment and revenge, and the competing nations down below doing exactly the same thing. "Vengeance is mine, says the Lord, and I will repay." And everybody else said it, too. It was a system of competing powers when it was not a system of powers cooperating, but always it was a system of powers. The first effect of Jesus' metaphor is to cancel that whole arrangement of things. Since all fatherhood, sourcehood, initiative, power, energy belong to God, they cannot belong to human beings. Power and the struggle for power simply do not exist in Jesus' new metaphor; or, if they do exist there, the scene of the temptations has shown they exist only as a lapse from the new paternal and filial way of living. In the new world of father and son there is only harmony. The poor are blessed *not* because poverty is a blessing but because the whole system that makes for poverty and riches, oppressors and oppressed, simply no longer exists.

Jesus speaks the Beatitudes from the perspective of his new metaphor, not from that of his cultural or religious tradition. He speaks these Beatitudes, then, from an experience of transcendent peace, that is, a peace that is differently constructed from the "peace" that occasionally reigns in the ordinary power world of human beings. Peace in the power world is the result of the temporary cessation of hostilities either by mutual agreement of roughly equal powers or by the conquest of the weak by the strong. But in the new world of the new metaphor, peace is a positive condition of things, an agreement from love or affinity instead of from exhaustion or fear. Here, then, the Beatitudes are not felt as paradoxical at all, but as simple givens. *Of course* those who are persecuted are blessed—not because they are persecuted, but because the economic or social or political or psychological causes of their persecution are simply less real, less permanent, less commanding, less significant, less present, and less potent than this all-encompassing fatherhood of God. Here there is no contradiction between mourning and being comforted because in this fatherhood nothing causes the mourning; all the causes of tears and therefore all need of comforting belong to another order, but here the whole order of the causes of tears is not so much refuted or corrected as simply swept away. Poverty and mourning are not swept away, but any universe of which they are an ordinary part is swept away. And so, within the terms of Jesus' own metaphor the Beatitudes are not felt as paradoxes but as self-evident and simple truths.

However, human beings do not usually belong to an order of surrenders and participations, but to an order of alliances of advantage, surrenders of advantage, wars of advantage, and even deaths of advantage. If Jesus looked out from his new metaphor which removed from people's lives all the dimensions of power and returned them to God's kind fatherhood, he must have seen a place where his Beatitudes would not seem so simple. In this other order to which human beings usually belong there is a price on everything, and consequently a rapid and heartless commerce. The order to which we belong is not happy.

Here, for example, virtually no one will die of entirely natural causes. Virtually everyone will die in some measure as the result of human causes, whether from war or a straightforward automobile accident or from the ruinous mixtures in artificial foods or from the unhealthy miracles of medical science. Here poverty and mourning have quite personal causes, and finding any blessedness in them would be the result either of the masochism of the weak or of the sadism of the strong. Here we will die from the caprices, not of an impersonal cosmos, but of a personal one, and not as the result of the indifference of powers that cannot see us but of the indifference of those close to us who can see us but will not. In this kind of world the Beatitudes are an outrageous paradox, a contradiction of conventional experience in the name of an unconventional one.

Your Turn   The Beatitudes express the way in which Jesus translated his experience of being related to an ultimate source (an unconventional experience) into activity that would transform the world of conventional morality to bring it into alignment with that source.

The emphasis in this exercise is on action—and how a vision might be translated into a consistent and coherent pattern of behavior. It is an exploration of how a dream becomes the core of an ethic. It offers a direct challenge to the premise that the world is divided into two irreconcileable camps: the doers and the dreamers.

The Beatitudes invite action. But they do not have the impersonal quality of laws. Each individual must find his or her own way of translating them into behavior, for they lack the specificity of "do this" or "don't do that."

They accept as givens Jesus' own vision and the realities you experience in your world—and without backing away in the slightest from either his vision or your world, we ask what they have to do with each other. We offer a way of struggling to find out how a dream might inform an ethic—of how a style of living and acting is rooted in Jesus' deepest sense of what life is all about.

The goal of this exercise is to relate the visions of Jesus specifically to one of the "worlds" you identified in the previous exercise. Choose one of those worlds that at this time most demands your time and energy, or the one you are most unsure of, or the one that you are most intrigued by. Jot down the details of your involvement in it.

This exercise may be done in several ways:

a. Read the whole text of the exercise. Then set it aside, close your eyes, and go through the stages. Then record your experience. Since the exercise is long you may need to read it over several times to become familiar with the various steps.

b. Or do it with someone else or with a group. One person can read the text while the other(s) are doing the meditation. The reader should not rush the group, and should allow plenty of silent time between the stages of the exercise.

c. Or do the exercise by yourself in sections, completing each section before moving on. If this is done it is important to spend time at the beginning of each section simply relaxing; these meditations cannot be done well if you are still thinking of the "mechanics" of the process. Do each step slowly. Allow the images to develop.

Stage One

Sit in a comfortable upright position, close your eyes, and relax. Put yourself into that "world" which you have singled out. Imagine your relationships, attitudes, problems—whatever gives that world its texture of experience. See yourself in that world.

Stage Two

Walk away from that world into a lovely green meadow on a quiet morning. You are alone. You can hear the sounds of the meadow. You are walking a path through the meadow which leads up the gentle slope of a mountain. You continue along as it ascends. You pause here and there as you wish, still going on with the climb. Before long you find yourself at the top. The air is clear, the sun shines brightly; it is warm and pleasant as you stand there.

Stage Three

You notice a pile of stones that have been carefully placed at the summit. They look like an ancient altar of some sort. Upon the rocks rests a large book lying open. Approach the book and read the text. At first the script looks strange, but you find you understand the words: "How blest are the poor in spirit: the reign of God is theirs. Blest too are the sorrowing; they shall be consoled. (Blest are the lowly; they shall inherit the land.) Blest are they who hunger and thirst for holiness; they shall have their fill. Blest are they who show mercy; mercy shall be theirs. Blest are the single-hearted for they shall see God. Blest too the peacemakers; they shall be called sons of God. Blest are those persecuted for holiness' sake; the reign of God is theirs. Blest are you when they insult you and persecute you and utter every kind of slander against you because of me. Be glad and rejoice, for your reward is great in heaven; they persecuted the prophets before you in the very same way." You have read the words. You stand a while at the top of the mountain, bathed in the light of this beautiful day.

Stage Four

The air is so sharp and pure that you can see great distances in all directions. You still hear the words of Jesus as you look down and see clearly the meadow from which you began your ascent to the mountain top. You can also see that world of yours which you left behind as you entered the meadow. You can observe carefully what is happening in that world, especially how the people there live and interact. In particular you can see the things there that bother or absorb you. You decide to leave the mountain and to re-enter that world. You will act out there the words you have heard here. What will you say? What will you do? What will be different?

Stage Five

Open your eyes now and think:

a. If you look at that world *from the perspective of the Beatitudes,* how is your own ordinary view of it changed?

b. If you look at the Beatitudes *from the perspective of that world* where you ordinarily live, how is your "mountain-top view" of them changed?

c. There is probably a pronounced tendency for one perspective to challenge or contradict the other. Jesus offered the Beatitudes as a constant challenge to the ordinary moral perspectives of the world—in other words, as an elaborate compressed conflict. Which one of the Beatitudes seems to apply especially strongly to you in your situation of moral conflict?

But the Beatitudes, so often admired for the simple beauty of their language and the gentleness of their sentiments, are paradoxical in still another way than we have considered so far. This poem to meekness is also, underneath, a threat. But these new ideas do not threaten us with punishments, as the old ones did. They threaten us with being merely meaningless and irrelevant in a universe that runs on different rules from our own. They charge us, in effect, with vanity rather than with venom, and dismiss us altogether instead of tying us to the stake. The Beatitudes constitute a dreadful judgment on humanity, worse than any that could be pronounced by a punishing power. For from the perspective of Jesus' new metaphor the ordinary human world is not so much evil as insane. That world's reaction of self-defense is, and must be, to consider the Beatitudes insane.

But there is still a further paradox in the Beatitudes. In the temptations Jesus has rejected power for himself and implicitly for everyone else. But he has reserved it for God. It is not gone. Power resides now in the father, not just preeminently as in most of the Old Testament, but absolutely and uniquely. It is still there, but it has gone underground. Or, at the very least, Jesus has yet to take up the question of whether to deny to the father himself the exercise of sheer power which he has denied to everyone else. Is his new vision *that* consistent?

If, then, the Beatitudes are underwritten not only by the *generosity* of the father but also by the *power* of the father, they imply threats of the old-fashioned kind. If the meek alone will be made happy, then everyone else will have to be made unhappy, and that includes a great many people. In this serene inaugural statement there is the first hint of a vehemence, not to say a violence, which will become more apparent as Jesus lives out his life under the inspiration of his metaphor.

Jesus speaks in explicit and implicit paradoxes because, having chosen a different metaphor from everyone else's, he cannot do otherwise. His hearers are thinking in the conventional terms; to speak to them at all he must use, at least sometimes, their terms. But his message is drastically different from the conventional wisdom. Therefore he must talk paradox and nonsense—or paradox and a new kind of sense. It is, then, a measure of the thoroughness with which he understands his way of existing that the first words he speaks to the world are also his first paradoxes.

The world of the father and son seems straight and simple at first. It will seem otherwise when it has been lived out.

Paradox is not only the style of Jesus' language. It is the essence of his life.

Father and Son:
Establishing the Metaphor

4. Conflicts in
the Guiding Image

(Matthew 5:17—12:30)

In the last chapter we concentrated on how Jesus' simple, coherent new way of existing, as expressed first in the metaphors of father and son, begins to seem more complex and even contradictory as the implications of the metaphors are further worked out in the Beatitudes. In the present chapter we will trace out the further contradictions which surface as Jesus thinks out and lives out the metaphor. Some of the conflicts will be external clashes between his vision and that of others. Some of them will be internal clashes within his vision itself.

In this chapter the following four groups of passages will be considered:
1. the Sermon on the Mount exclusive of the Beatitudes (Chapters 5-7)
2. the healing activities of Jesus (Chapters 8 and 9)
3. Jesus' sermon to the disciples (Chapter 10)
4. the open hostility between Jesus and others (Chapters 11 and 12).

We have a speech, actions, a speech, actions. The four passages in sequence are the record of Jesus' fundamental attempt, in both words and deeds, to live out the metaphor he has chosen as the definition of his life. His metaphor of father and son, like all paradigms, is intended to simplify life and to reduce it to order and predictability. It is intended as an affirmation that there is an intelligible structure to all experience and that the human mind and imagination are up to the task of finding it. The four passages show Jesus thinking out and living out the new order of things implied in his new metaphor. The enterprise begins auspiciously in the exquisite Sermon on the Mount, where the fatherhood of God and the brotherhood of man occupy the center of vision, but as Jesus moves more in the world, he encounters more and more opposition from without. He finds that his metaphor is as much a source of social conflict as it is of personal inspiration. He begins to find, too, that even apart from external conflict, the metaphor is not entirely a source of harmony. He begins to find conflicts inherent within it. Scarcely felt at first, they gradually become so powerful they almost tear his central vision apart.

Your Turn   There is a good reason why symbols which are intended to represent and to stimulate unity among people have a way of turning into rather lethal sources of division. The altar in the Temple at Jerusalem, which Jesus mentions in his Sermon, was such a symbol. Designed to unify a nation, it became instead a sign of its internal separations; designed to signify the union and harmony between God and humanity, it became too often a sign of the grief which separated them.

Before we explore that symbol further, let us look at how the same kind of thing happens with our own symbols. Images and metaphors which mean one thing for us may provoke a very different reaction in others.

What in your experience can properly be called a symbol of unity? We are suggesting two and invite you to continue to list a number of other symbols of unity in the space below:

Symbols of Unity

the national flag

the language you speak

How do they symbolize unity?
To the right of each symbol write how you see it as a symbol of unity.

How do these symbols or images or metaphors of unity also serve as symbols of division, discord, or separation? Go back over each of the symbols and write in the space below how it is a symbol of division.

These symbols, then, are ambiguous. Metaphors that stand for reconciliation and understanding are the same ones that stand for animosity and prejudice. Why is this so for the symbols you have chosen?

The altar at Jerusalem was such a symbol. For one part of the nation it was a symbol of unity of faith and culture—but at the same time it was a concrete reminder that there were other members of the Israelite nation who did not come to this altar to worship. The sign of their being cut off and looked down upon was the very same altar that for the others expressed faith and national purpose.

But symbols of unity are meant to do more than signify. They often quite clearly are designed to stimulate some specific kind of activity. They appeal to minds and hearts, but the effective symbol stirs people to act. And if the symbol is well chosen it will lead to a kind of action that promotes the kind of unity indicated by the symbol.

What kind of unifying behavior is provoked by the symbols you have chosen? Go back over your list and write below the actions that your symbols do actually provoke.

If on the one hand symbols which are intended to evoke unity do provoke behavior that is unifying, they can then, in so far as they prove to be symbols of discord, provoke activity which is divisive. What type of divisive behavior is provoked by each of the symbols you have chosen?

The altar at Jerusalem was such an inspiration to action. It was designed as a place of worship—a place where the faithful of Israel would go to offer sacrifices to reconcile themselves with their God. Something was to be *done* there. The prophets and Jesus recognized that it was a symbol designed to effect a change in one's whole being and flow through into one's daily activity. It would be the charge of the prophetic tradition that activity which took place only at the altar was at least hypocritical and more probably an occasion for national disaster.

The altar in Jerusalem was even more a special kind of symbol for Jesus. His father was father to all, and the altar in his father's house which evoked an experience of unity for him ought to provoke behavior of a universal kind. So not only would one who worshipped at that altar and expressed harmony with that God be expected to reconcile oneself with one's brother, but such reconciliation would necessarily be extended to one's opposition, even to one's enemies.

What kind of unity do your symbols evoke?

Go back over all and decide if they do evoke a universal or a more limited type of unity. When you have done that, in the following space describe also the kind of universalist or particularist kind of behavior they provoke. (If your list does not contain any symbols that evoke a kind of universal unity write out the name of some that might do so. Describe how they evoke that kind of unity for you and what behavior they provoke.)

There are, then, two points to be made about unity symbols:

1. Unity symbols seem to *evoke* a sense of full unity on all levels of experience, but often really stand for much less than that. They tend to be hypocritical.
2. Unity symbols of themselves do not necessarily *provoke* high ethical behavior; they can easily also provoke very narrow ethical behavior.

A third notion is implied in the first two:

3. It is the person using the symbol who determines what kind of unity it evokes and what kind of ethical response it provokes. The symbol does not interpret itself.

Rather clearly, Jesus is taking a unity symbol—the altar—and making an active decision about what it means (see point 3, above). He is interpreting it as implying an ethic of effective universal reconciliation within the human race (see point 2), and as allowing no limitations, qualifications, hesitations, or hypocrisies (see point 1).

He knew full well of course that in fact the altar did not stand for that at all to most people. To the priestly caste it held little or no ethical implications (point 2) and was in competition with all other places of worship and all other ideals of worship (point 1). The prophetic tradition tended to agree, and concluded from that that the symbol itself was utterly worthless; all that mattered was right behavior, not right symbolism.

But Jesus accepts the symbol as something that stood as an ideal of unity, while insisting that the unity must be deep enough to embrace all levels of experience and broad enough to embrace the whole range of humanity.

By standing for that kind of unity, he paradoxically cuts himself off from most of his contemporaries. It has always been the fate of the universalist to stand alone, and of the person who calls for unity to divide as well as to unite.

In the four passages we will now study, there is a remarkable progression from the simple to the complex, from the harmonious to the discordant, from the logical to the contradictory, from the peaceful to the violent. For example, early in the first of the passages Jesus says, "What I say to you is: everyone who grows angry with his brother shall be liable to judgment" (5:22), but near the end of the last of the passages he says, "I have come to set a man at odds with his father, a daughter with her mother, a daughter-in-law with her mother-in-law: in short, to make a man's enemies those of his own household" (10:35). Something has brought out the negative possibilities in a vision which, at the first, seemed filled only with hope. If we have gone from the family as image of reconciliation in the earlier passage to the family as image of strife in the later one, and if the guiding metaphor in both cases is still that of life under God as father, something drastic has been happening to our sense of what God's fatherhood implies for us. At first it is the power to harmonize, but it becomes more and more the power to divide. The metaphor, at first so clarifying, confounds.

We will discuss the four passages in sequence and watch the progress of the complication.

The Sermon on the Mount (Chapters 5-7)

The first passage, the Sermon on the Mount, is a kind of hymn to life as it will be when God is established as the universal father. It will be a world free of conflicts, full of reconciliations. Jesus begins (5:13ff) by providing us with a brief catalogue of the situations of hostility and complexity in which people so often find themselves: worshippers of God who nevertheless have quarrels with others, married people who nevertheless commit adultery, married people who divorce each other, people who swear elaborate oaths instead of relying on simple trust. Jesus provides a counter-image for all these complex situations, that of turning the other cheek.

It is not clear *why* we should go to such lengths to bring peace until we realize that Jesus finds in God's fatherhood the source of this ethic of simple harmony. If metaphors imply programs of action, this metaphor implies a program of the pacification and simplification of all human relationships. Jesus bases his ideas about what human behavior should be on how, in some ways, we are *like* and how in other ways we are *unlike* the father (Chapters 6 and 7). In other words, he implicitly argues to our behavior from the metaphor which defines us, the metaphor which operates as the context within which our actions will take place.

His first argument is essentially: Be *like* your father, that is, hidden, sincere, and forgiving (6:1-18).

His second argument is essentially: Be *unlike* your father, that is, be dependent, pass no judgments, and ask trustingly for whatever you need. Independence, the right to judge, and the power to fulfill needs, belong to the father, not to the children (6:19-7:12).

The very core of Jesus' argument lies in the way he understands the metaphor of fatherhood: "Would one of you hand his son a stone when he asks for a loaf, or a poisonous snake when he asks for a fish?" (7:9-10) This is his most explicit statement so far about what fatherhood means, and it suggests no paradoxes or darker possibilities. If God is taken for father, everything harmonizes. Jesus concludes his statement of the implications of God's fatherhood for humanity's moral life with a firm judgment against those who fail to live out his words, and an equally firm judgment in favor of those who do (7:15-29).

Your Turn　　Jesus repeatedly stresses the private, almost secret, nature of one's relationship with the father. The image he uses to suggest the kind of secrecy he has in mind is that of going to one's room and simply closing the door. That room with the closed door is a direct analogy for privacy and intimacy.

Everyone has had the experience of a deliberately chosen privacy, in which one chooses not to be seen or heard by anyone else. Describe to yourself an instance or two during the last week when you literally or figuratively "shut the door" on everyone else in order to be unseen and unheard.

The kind of privacy Jesus had in mind is probably not quite like the one you have just described. For him, what we normally call privacy or secrecy is simply another, quieter way of being seen and heard. In effect, for Jesus there is no such thing as privacy. There is only a choice about who will see or hear us. Being public means the choice of being seen and heard by other people; being private, the choice of being visible only to God.

Name several times in your life when the simple phenomenon of being looked at by another was comforting and comfortable.

Of course it is not always like that. Name several times in your life when the opposite was true, and being looked at by another was painful or embarrassing.

Being seen by another can be one of the most quietly happy or one of the most grimly demeaning experiences imaginable. Yet for Jesus just that condition of being constantly seen is the *normal* one. How can this be so? It may not seem so far-fetched if you stop to realize that in his remarks on being seen in private and rewarded in private there is an implied metaphor.

When in your life was it normal to be constantly seen, and seen in private—seen, that is, in everything you did, whether it was publicly acceptable or not, seen in such a way that it was always comfortable no matter what you were doing?

The chances are very strong that you cannot remember any such time at all, for if it ever existed for you it was probably a long time ago. But you can still see it happening sometimes for some other people. When was the last time you saw anything like this?

The last time we saw it was in very young children, for whom there is virtually no privacy at all, whose lives are spent in a constant but generally comfortable visibility, who do all sorts of things in the sight of their mothers that in just a year or two they will be ashamed to do at all, except in the most complete secrecy. In very early childhood there is a time of being constantly and quietly seen, and in that time being seen is—or at least can be—almost the same thing as being happy, for it is the evidence of being loved.

Of course the look could be and often is embarrassing and even accusing. The comfort easily turns into shame. The way children are looked at will make them feel either confident of their essential rightness or more and more uncomfortable with the way they have been made to feel.

Jesus implicitly proposes, then, as the model for a person's life with God the condition of a very young child with its mother. It is the condition of being constantly but comfortably seen, and of being rewarded with love no matter whether we "deserve" it or not.

Jesus does not draw attention to the fact that that is also the condition of absolute vulnerability, so that, if the look turns harsh or cold, there are no defenses against it. It can be the condition of the most crushing shame, if the eyes that see should also be the eyes that accuse.

Are you now ever like that small child: seen by eyes that can make you feel entirely comfortable but that, if they change their expression, can make you feel terribly uneasy?

Maybe only lovers can answer yes to that question.

In any case, Jesus lets the matter of being totally visible to another seem serenely uncomplicated. For him, at the beginning of his career, the darker possibilities in that condition do not show up. The life of the child of this motherly father is spent in the sight of the simplest and most comfortable love. It will not, of course, always be so simple.

Even though the image of the room may have its own potential ambiguities (as do almost all of Jesus' images), he nevertheless seems to be implying rather strongly in this passage that everyone has his or her own personal space in which to be "seen" by the father-God in a particular and intimate way. Like the prophets of old, he implies that the intimate relationship of the father and the children is not confined to temples.

The "room" Jesus speaks of can and should be looked at in its broadest, most metaphorical sense as that time and place which each person can claim as especially his or her own, the time and place of one's most personal visions and of the images by which they are expressed. The remainder of this exercise is intended to help you to reflect upon your own personal images of harmony and peace with your ultimate source.

Give your imagination free play to recreate that "room," that time or place in which you experience the kind of harmony Jesus speaks of. What does that "room" look like? Where is it? How is it painted? decorated? furnished? What does it look out on?

This "room" is entirely *yours*. Allow yourself in imagination to be in this "room." What is the color, the sound, the music, the fragrance, the shape, the height, the texture of this "room"? Become well acquainted with the whole range of your personal imagery.

Draw on these images to help you answer some questions about yourself:

What quality or feeling do you most clearly experience in that "room"? Peace? compassion? something entirely different?

Is there some actual place or time in which you experience this quality most vividly?

Is there some person in whose presence you experience it?

What prevents you from experiencing it in your daily life, in your ordinary times and places?

What can you do to bring this quality more into your life?

The image of one's private "room" is one of a whole range of highly personal images Jesus used to express his own personal experience of ultimate harmony and to suggest the possibility of a similar experience for us. A great part of the Sermon on the Mount is devoted to helping us take such images seriously, for they have the power to put us in touch with the deeper dimensions of ourselves.

It is all that one would expect from someone who has had a great vision. It is his credo that in this vision there is power enough to inaugurate a new world, free of the human-wrought miseries of the old. But this brave new world of harmonies, even here in its freshest statement, contains images of an unexpected violence and rending. Jesus uses these images without comment, and apparently without stopping to notice how out of character with the rest of his speech they are. As a particularly vivid example, in the midst of his talk urging reconciliation with one's brother and harmony between spouses and love for one's enemies, he suddenly recommends irreconciliation, disharmony, and hatred *within oneself:* "If your right eye is your trouble, gouge it out and throw it away...; if your right hand is your trouble, cut it off and throw it away..." (5:29-30). He does not seem to notice the extreme contrast between the integrated social life he portrays in the surrounding passages and the internal civil war he pictures here. Nor apparently does he seem to notice the conflict between this saying of his in which salvation depends on our breaking ourselves apart and that other saying of his to the effect that "A town or household split into factions cannot last for long" (12:25). The significant thing is not that they are paradoxes—we have already pointed out Jesus' acceptance of that—but that they are paradoxes of which Jesus himself seems to become increasingly aware. They suggest a breach *within* Jesus' vision itself. There is more to his metaphor than lies on the surface. Something about the father leads not only to harmony but to division.

One can wonder in reading the Sermon on the Mount if Jesus really wanted to be taken seriously. The preacher of blessedness turns quickly into a prophet of doom and curses. The gentle Jew calls for a variety of violent reprisals for the offender. Jesus the gentle is also Jesus the brutal.

Brutality: Gentleness—the followers of Jesus have both qualities in very uneasy combinations and with disastrous consequences. Students of the history of Christianity have much to wince at in the annals of piety and bloodshed that fill the pages of books that are not all *ancient* history. From the Catholic Church to the 30 Years' War to Martin Luther's crushing of the peasants to the woes of Northern Ireland in our own day, Christian history has seen its full share of wars between those who think of themselves as the sons and daughters of God and the brothers and sisters of Jesus.

And somehow this Jesus who now speaks on the mount is invoked by the pious and bloodthirsty alike, both of whom act in his name.

Your Turn   What is Jesus saying here? We assume he means to be taken seriously. We also assume that the violence committed in his name is as abhorrent to him as to any observer of the past and present history of the Christian peoples. We do assume that Jesus, therefore, is serious when in the middle of this sermon he says love your enemy and be perfect as your heavenly father is perfect. And yet he speaks in images of great violence.

The exercise which follows is designed to present a *model* for examining the violent words of Jesus—to find, then, a way of avoiding the common experience of just remaining puzzled and of discarding words that are there in the gospel and that cannot simply be passed over.

The model we have chosen is derived from Jesus' insistent use of a left/right orientation. We are intrigued by the possibilities which open up when we look at left/right as metaphor. The metaphorical model may help us to find a way to accept the violence of Jesus' words and through them come to realize what an important contribution they make to a life of true peace.

Curiously, in most of the passages referring to our left or right sides, Jesus sees the right side as the offender. It does wrong; therefore cut it off or pluck it out. Even when it is doing something honorable, e.g., giving alms, it has to be constrained from boasting about it to the left side, as though boasting were its normal way of acting.

Why is the right side seen as the offender, when the customs and languages of many cultures have taken *right* to mean *correct, lawful, just, honest, moral? Left,* in the same languages, is the source of the bizarre, the clumsy, the dark, the evil, and—in ancient heraldry—of the illegitimate. In English we inherit the Latin *sinister* and the French *gauche,* thereby keeping alive this very peculiar prejudice.

Jesus in seeing the right side as offender (and the left as offended) seems to be trying to counter-balance the bias that has made one side of the human person more acceptable than the other. Jesus' strong words can be seen as a measure of the violence such bias may actually have done to people in many cultures, since it takes an equal and opposite violence to "correct" it.

Violence may seem a strong word here, but psychologists today have more and more come to believe that the results of dis-integrating the left and right sides of the body (and, as we will see in a moment, of the brain) can be very harmful. For the left and right sides contribute different dimensions of experience and activity to the life of human beings, and without one or the other we can hardly be said to be full personalities.

Current theory even holds that we have two brains, one left, one right:

It seems more than coincidental that the values of society seem to favor the talents of the brain's right-handed (left) hemisphere over its left-handed (right) hemisphere. We need only look at school budgets to find out where our main values lie. And who is thought to be more valuable—the city planner, or the urban poet?

But mythology tells us that the god Odin had to put out his right eye before he could drink of the spring of poetry and wisdom. And the gospel says that when Jesus will enter the final kingdom he will sit at the right hand of the father; in other words, he will have the father on his *left!* Perhaps, then, it is more significant than at first appears that in the passages of the Sermon on the Mount he seems to favor the orientation of the left side as somehow less offensive to his vision of life than that of the right.

Probably no one is free from every kind of bias that would favor one side of the body over the other. If you are right-handed, what is your attitude toward those who are left-handed?

If you are left-handed, what is your attitude toward those who are right-handed?

The two following exercises are designed to help you explore the left-right question in your own experience. Read the directions through, and then sit back with your eyes closed and go through the first exercise.

1. Sit comfortably in a chair with both feet on the floor. Put your hands on your legs; do not fold your hands together. Relax. Breathe evenly.
2. Close your eyes and imagine a line extending from the crown of your head downward, dividing your body into left and right halves.
3. Now focus attention on your right side, noticing the way each of its parts feels to you. Give yourself plenty of time for this. Then ask yourself the question, What color is my right side?
4. Repeat step three for your left side.
   What color was your right side? Write it here.

What color was your left side? Write it here.

Take a crayon of the first color in your right hand and a crayon of the second in your left. On this page let both hands make random designs. Try not to exercise too much conscious control over the designs they make.

Now do a personal analogy fantasy on the right hand color. Answer such questions as:

- How do I feel about my shape? Where am I tense or relaxed?
- How well do I like my color? What are the best and worst things about being this color?
- How do I feel about the left-hand shape? Does it have anything I want?
- How well do I like the other color?

When you are finished, go back and do the same exercise over again, identifying now with the left-hand color.

Personal Analogy

Right-hand color   Left-hand color

The culture which *sets* meanings on "leftness" and "rightness" tends to impose them on its members. We have noted that science and psychology have begun to use those categories in describing the hemispheres of the brain and corresponding types of thinking.

From the left/right exercises you have done what are the principal characteristics you have found for:

left?   right?

How are the characteristics you found like/unlike those in the viewpoint of traditional cultures? How are they like/unlike the left/right model of psychology?

You have been reflecting on your own images and feelings about left and right. But that division is more than just personal to you. It extends through a great many dimensions of our culture as well. Listed below are a number of things in the public world. Classify each on the basis of whether they are "left" or "right," using:

1. the conventional concept of left/right and/or
2. your own experience of what is "left/right" and/or
3. the left/right psychological model

	Right	**Left**
Institutions that are		
Mechanical things that are		
Emotions that are		
Buildings in your community that are		

                                                        Right   **Left**

Articles of clothing that are

Nations of the world that are

Men you know who are

Women you know who are

Add your own categories to the list:

     In each of the above how could the right be seen as a stumbling block for the left? What would it mean to cut off the right side?

     In none of these exercises is there an implication that one side is better than the other. They are two sides of a whole. But they are seldom really taken that way. One is preferred over the other.

What wounds can you see in your world that could be the result of splitting the right and left sides of experience?

What wounds can you see in yourself that could be the result of splitting the right and left sides of experience?

Keeping your answers in mind, how would you interpret Matthew 5:43-48: "You have heard the commandment, 'You shall love your countryman but hate your enemy.' My command to you is: love your enemies, pray for your persecutors. This will prove that you are sons of your heavenly Father, for his sun rises on the bad and the good, he rains on the just and the unjust. If you love those who love you, what merit is there in that? Do not tax collectors do as much? And if you greet your brothers only, what is so praiseworthy about that? Do not pagans do as much? In a word, you must be made perfect as your heavenly Father is perfect." Remember that *perfect* means *that which is whole*.

Jesus himself, in his reflection on the right and left sides, may well be trying to correct an overemphasis on the right by means of an overemphasis on the left. Still, his approach, though intended to bring about a harmony, has the unintended effect of replacing one disharmony with another. The central vision of his great Sermon on the Mount is of a world at one with itself because at one with God, but the metaphors he uses to express that vision are sometimes paradoxically violent and disordered, as when he would pluck out the right eye and cut off the right hand.

It is not easy to be a reconciler. Perhaps that is because the act of reconciliation itself has a violent dimension to it. It *disrupts* disorder.

We have pointed out the unexplained schism within Jesus' vision by dwelling on the images of the altar, the closed room, and our left and right sides. There is also an external one which is equally unexplained. The man who "builds his house" on the rock of Jesus' words apparently does so in the expectation of fierce winds and floods (7:24). The Sermon on the Mount begins with talk of harmonies and ends in a raging storm—and storms are, classically, manifestations of the power and majesty of God. Is there a hint here that the God, who is experienced as father, can also be experienced as a chaos of wind and a battering of rain? Jesus seems to be allowing the darker side of his originally lucid vision to surface. The first of the four passages we are considering thus suggests a disquieting split, not simply between Jesus and anyone else, but within Jesus' own universe. His metaphor makes paradoxes for others; and it makes them for him, too.

The Ministry of Jesus (8:1—9:38)

The second set of passages we are considering suggests much the same thing, only this time through deeds and the consequences of deeds rather than through words and images. Once again we have the explicit conflict *between* Jesus and his opponents—a thing he seems to have expected from the beginning—and the hidden but emerging conflict *within* his own message and, by implication at least, within his own imagination. Now in deeds, as before in images, Jesus suggests something problematic within God, or rather, within his own metaphor for God. There is a doubleness about "the father" that begins to show.

At the end of his Sermon, Jesus "descends from the mountain," that place where traditionally revelations are first received privately and then given to the public. He comes down to apply the revelation; in this case that means to apply the metaphor of God-father to the world of human beings. In his first several encounters (Chapter 8), Jesus brings the presence and power of the father-God into successful, beneficial contact with human beings, lepers, the Roman centurion's slave, Peter's mother-in-law, the possessed—they all experience him and the presence of his father as healing and reconciling, just as he presented himself in the Sermon.

But just as the initial promise of the Sermon seems fulfilled, Jesus himself introduces what seems, after all, an unnecessary harshness, a gratuitous insult. Impressed with Jesus, a young man desires to follow him but has first to bury his father. Jesus, now unhealing, now wounding, tells him to "let the dead bury their dead" (8:22). One cannot help noticing that "the dead" here is a father, therefore along with Abraham a source of potential competition to Jesus' central vision and metaphor. God's fatherhood appears, for just a moment, to be downright ominous. But immediately after this incident, Jesus again appears as one bringing peace from on high; having caused a storm within the young man, he calms one on the open sea—restoring thereby an aspect of peace to the God who is revealed in storms. The main impact of Jesus' actions so far is therefore to demonstrate the father's effect as pacifier of a warring world and healer of a wounded world. But the father's *other* effect has been felt, likewise, at least by one young man.

And there are other people in this second group of passages for whom the presence and power of the father and his son are not altogether benign. Jesus encounters two demoniacs, that is, two men who are made instruments of some spirit other than God (8:28). He does the reconciling thing: he casts out the demons. But then he shows an odd compassion for the demons themselves by letting them inhabit a herd of pigs. And here Jesus has done an unreconciling thing. A Jew might think a herd of pigs a fit place for demons, but the herdsmen here are not Jews, and the pigs are their livelihood. To comfort the demons, Jesus, with surprising insensitivity, bankrupts the owners. For it was the *whole* herd that ran into the sea. The people of the nearby town do not detect in Jesus any of that sublime peace and reconciliation we have heard in the Sermon on the Mount. If this is the presence and power of the father, these people clearly would prefer his absence, and say so. Jesus is beginning to experience for himself what surely God must have experienced from the beginning, namely, that there is a perplexing doubleness about his impact on humanity.

Immediately after destroying the herd of pigs he cures a paralytic, surely an unexceptionable act (9:2ff). But he does not leave it at that. This manifestation of the father's kind power is tied up with something else not quite so kind. If his healing the man seems a benign application of God's power, his forgiving the man's sin can only be seen as a direct usurpation of God's power. Jesus is asking the Jews to believe that all of a sudden God is sharing one of his most important powers, the power to forgive. In other words, the jealous and absolute father is suddenly sharing his fatherhood, the god his godhood. It is a notion Jesus himself has condemned repeatedly, this usurpation of the prerogatives of God. And now he assumes them himself. There is a new and especially problematic doubleness here within the person and message of Jesus; is he son, or is he father? Toward the father he acts as a son, but toward God's other children he acts more and more like a father. Simplicity is being lost in a confusion of functions, one far deeper than the confusion about the relationship of Abraham to God. This confusion will return.

There are more suggestions of the increasingly problematic quality of the presence of Jesus. It is not surprising, of course, that the Pharisees find his association with tax collectors obnoxious (9: 11). These are, after all, practically an extension of the Roman army of occupation. Jesus explains that his business is with sinners, but why so conspicuously with precisely those sinners whom not God but his compatriots will find the most objectionable politically? Why confuse the separate issues of sin and politics? Consider in this connection the passage immediately following in which John the Baptizer's disciples appear every bit as scandalized over Jesus' failure to fast (9:14) as were the Pharisees over his association with traitors. It is almost as if Jesus cannot help giving offense to everyone, and offense for no very clear purpose.

He makes only one attempt to explain this drift toward complexity, confusion, and contradiction. He explains the situation, typically, by means of a metaphor. He says, "People do not pour new wine into old wineskins. If they do, the skins burst, the wine spills out, and the skins are ruined. No, they pour new wine into new wineskins, and in that way both are preserved" (9:17). He sees himself and his message as a new wine. He is therefore putting a metaphor onto a metaphor, explaining an earlier analogy by means of still another. Thus God is to Jesus as a father is to a son, and they together are to the world as new wine to an old wineskin.

What is interesting about this second analogy is that with no effort at all it can be taken in a double sense. New wine needs a new container: the feeling of the metaphor is of something fresh, hopeful, clear, clean; in short, desirable. And of course old skins sag and are ugly and weak and old wines are unclear. That is one sense in which we can take the metaphor—as complimentary to the father and the son. The other way of taking it, of course, is that new wine is not drinkable and is therefore practically unsaleable. It is an acid and will quite ungraciously destroy its leather container after one use, and until it has *ceased* to be a new wine it will be merely harsh and sickening. If Jesus is explaining the effect of his first metaphor by means of this second one, we are left to wonder in which sense to understand the words. It is clear that there is something at work here other than just the brighter side of all these metaphors.

Sermon to the Disciples (Chapter 10)

Indeed, the third set of passages here being considered shows him to be thinking in two different ways about the central metaphor of his life. He sends his disciples out into the world, but before doing so he gives them his reading of it. He says they will encounter the same conflicts with others as he has himself but urges on them that same tranquil faith he has urged before. The idea is still that God is the father, therefore do not worry. But he says it in a curious way: "Are not two sparrows sold for next to nothing? Yet not a single sparrow falls to the ground without your Father's consent. As for you, every hair of your head has been counted; so do not be afraid of anything. You are worth more than an entire flock of sparrows" (10:29-30). This is not quite the same as before, when he had said that fathers always gave their children bread and fish, never stones and scorpions. Here is quite a different idea of a father as one who watches the sparrows fall, and who not only watches the fall but who wills it. The intended effect of appealing to God's fatherhood is to inspire confidence in the disciples, but the opposite effect is at least as plausible. For here the father does not save; he destroys.

Your Turn
Everything in our present chapter points to a growing complication within Jesus' view of a person's life with God, and the analogy of the birds is no exception to that trend.

To see what the complication means for the unworried, relaxed faith in the fatherly providence of God which Jesus recommends to his disciples, do what Jesus suggests and put yourself in the position of the birds of the air. Think of some kind of bird you are reasonably familiar with and join forces and feelings with it. What bird is it? Describe it carefully.

Close your eyes and imagine yourself as the bird. Give yourself plenty of time to take on its form, its way of moving and seeing, its entire range of activity.

Stage One

It is the dawn of a quiet day in early spring. Everything is coming to life in the new warmth. You awaken to see and feel—what?

Stage Two

The sun climbs in the sky. The air itself seems alive. Describe your relationship to the air, the easy and unworried way you interact with it, what it offers you, what you give to it. It is your friend, the element in which you live. It is the thing you know best. No other creature on the planet knows the air better than you. Tell the air what you feel toward it.

Stage Three

But something is happening in the spring air. It still feels alive, but in a terribly different way. It moves more roughly. It has a darker quality. You seem to be pushed and hit by invisible powers. Very quickly the world of your friend has turned into a confusion of wind, rain, lightning, thunder. The air is still the element in which you live. Tell the air what you feel toward it. *(Note:* This part of the personal analogy can be helped along by listening to the selection called "Spring" in *Sonic Seasonings* by Walter Carlos, or any other music suggestive of storms.)

Stage Four

Exhausted, you cannot continue. Your wings will not carry you. Your friend allows you to fall. Now the air is the element in which you die. Tell the air what you feel toward it *now.*

Stage Five

Everything is still now. Listen to the absolute silence within you as you lie on the ground. That is the air's last gift to you. And you no longer have anything to say in return.

Jesus proposes the birds of the air as the models of an unworried faith. But he allows the simple, poetic image to become more troublesome, for he sees that the birds that trust also are the birds that are allowed to fall. Faith has to do with ultimate trust, even death-embracing trust, not with any kind of release from the conditions of an earthly life. Once again, Jesus goes beyond the commonplace into the heart of paradox.

Nor does Jesus stop there. He continues in the same vein, emphasizing that the words *father* and *son* do not contain meanings only of life and confidence. They are the names also of betrayal, hatred and fear: "A man's enemies [will be] those of his own household" (10:36). As long as Jesus is thinking directly about God, he takes *father* in a positive sense; if necessary he even forces such a sense. But when he takes the word by itself in its literal sense in the human world he takes it more and more negatively. Sooner or later Jesus will have to put these two mutually antagonistic points of view together and feel the force of the contradiction at the heart of his governing idea. But that time is not yet.

Jesus the Contradictor (Chapters 11 and 12)

In the fourth set of passages we are considering, Jesus experiences even more intensely the external conflicts between himself and his opponents. He curses the towns that will not receive him, but then praises God for hiding his message from them—an odd thing for the father to do, but Jesus does not dwell on that (Chapter 11).

He then (Chapter 12) provokes fights with the Pharisees by breaking the Sabbath laws in highly visible ways. Apparently all the events of this chapter about the Sabbath are seen as happening on the same day. That would mean that on a single day, in view of everyone, Jesus breaks the Sabbath laws by (1) plucking ears of grain with his followers, (2) healing the man with a withered hand, (3) walking more than the lawful distance and encouraging others to do the same, (4) healing those who broke the law by following him, (5) healing blind and dumb demoniacs. So he deliberately intensifies the external conflict.

But what of the conflict within his metaphor itself? The original purpose of the metaphor of fatherhood was to bring order and simplicity into life, to clean up the incoherent mess that life is when there is no organized idea to it. But the metaphor itself had turned many-sided and contradictory, as *father* has become a word for both dependability and treachery. Jesus seems to be reflecting on just this sort of problem when, apropos of nothing in particular, he muses about the unclean spirit who is cast out from a man and wanders while leaving the man free (12:43-45). Eventually the spirit returns bringing seven other spirits with him, and the cleansed man is once again inhabited by ghosts, the simplified and orderly man is once again complicated and in disarray, and the peaceful man experiences once again the war within. Jesus, too, has cast out the demon of confusion by the cleansing power of his great metaphor, the fatherhood of God. And he, too, has seen the conflict which he had cast out by the front door return by the rear door. Still, in the closing passage of this dilemma-ridden series, he reaffirms his idea. He points to his disciples and says that they are his mothers and his brothers because they, like him, are one with his father (12:49-50). He says it as though he had never known the family words to refer to anything but the surest love and loyalty.

But of course, in some other part of his soul, he knows otherwise. The metaphor he has chosen to simplify and organize his own life and that of all humanity is beginning to show its power to confound more and more. Jesus has proposed the life of children of the father as the solution to the ageless problems of the human race, but the solution contains a new set of difficulties. In the four passages we have just considered, *father* is not only a word of pure goodness and kindness. *Father* is the word, too, of anger, vehemence, and even caprice. To call God father is, then, to say both that he is the solution to humanity's old woes and simultaneously that he is himself the new problem that needs to be solved. His is a heavy blessing, and Jesus will have to carry the weight of it to the end.

God is the solution *and* the problem.

5. Liberation vs. Confinement: Conflicts in Jesus' Images of the Kingdom

(Matthew 13:1—16:20)

Matthew has presented Jesus as the man of paradox *par excellence,* and by the time he has reached the midpoint of his gospel where we are now he has also suggested why Jesus is so. It is because God—or rather, the metaphor of father for God—is full of paradox, bright competing with dark, clear with murky. Thus God—or father—is both solution *and* problem.

At the very outset of Jesus' career he encountered three figures who implicitly posed three distinct versions of the same central dilemma to him. They were John the Baptizer, Satan, and the Pharisees. The dilemma they confronted Jesus with, in their various ways, was simply that his metaphor was paradoxical.

John and Satan raised the dilemma one way. Satan proposed that being "the son" should result in an inner feeling of real power, personal vitality, and independence. John proposed that being "son" was a hollow claim; that God could spawn whole generations out of a pile of rocks; that sons were not what mattered, only fathers did, and that fathers did not matter either; only God did. Satan and John in effect spoke to Jesus about two opposite sides of his metaphor, one taking it in a liberating sense, the other in a confining sense.

This first of the three problems Jesus has to deal with in his metaphor is the subject of the present chapter. The other two will be the subjects of the following two chapters.

The chapter just concluded suggests that the metaphors by which one establishes the terms of his or her life probably always have negative and disquieting possibilities within them. The metaphors are originally chosen for other, brighter reasons, and only with experience reveal their hidden darknesses. This point is no doubt true, but it should not be allowed to obscure the primary fact that it is by making metaphor—by asking again and again, "What is this life of mine *like?*"—that meaning finally emerges. Being free to play with metaphor in a sustained experience at once fanciful and grave is indispensable for any significant reflection on the meaning and purpose of one's life. To make and remake metaphors is an act of freedom. It is the result of inner freedom, for only a free person can let go of habits and try on new ways of seeing things. It is also the cause of an increased freedom, for as making and remaking metaphors becomes a habit of mind, such freedom becomes more familiar and more delightful.

In the passages to be considered presently, Jesus appears as one fully at home with this kind of freedom. He shows not only what he thinks but how he thinks, and the how involves the freedom to play. After the passages which show him, so to speak, playing with metaphors for the life of human beings with God (13:1-52), there is a sequence of scenes (13:53—16:20) in which various kinds of people try to make metaphors for him and for what he is doing. Their ability or their failure to tolerate him seems directly related to their own tolerance for playing with metaphor, that is, with different ways of answering the question, "What is this man *like?*" In the second set of passages, then, Jesus himself becomes the thing to be interpreted, the thing to be metaphorized.

Jesus Plays with Metaphors

The first set of passages (13:1-52) begins in an almost comic way. The scene has Jesus sitting beside the sea, probably staring off in thought toward the horizon. "Great crowds" gather to see and hear the famous man, who escapes to a boat and, again, sits there silent off shore. He looks at the crowds and the crowds look at him. The silence must be complete, the suppressed excitement intense. He is going to speak. What will the great man say, so dramatically enthroned on his floating stage? "One day a farmer went out sowing," he says. (Yes, yes?) "Some seeds the birds ate, some the sun scorched, some the weeds choked, and some grew." (Yes? Yes?) It is an interesting beginning, rhetorically sound, because it appeals to what the audience already knows and promises to lead them by indirection, discreetly, toward something exciting or controversial. It is even a perfect beginning, a model for orators on how to introduce a great idea by the homeliest and most accessible means. But—and here is the comedy—this is not the introduction. It is the whole speech. The buildup of crowds and boats and dramatic pauses was all for this, this commonplace, this brief commonplace, this least provocative of all possible commonplaces. The anticlimax is made even more abortive by his solemnizing the little speech with the fierce words, "Let everyone heed what he hears!" as though something enormous has just been proclaimed. Apparently that is the end of the matter, and we are left to imagine everyone going home, muttering to themselves.

The disciples realize that Jesus has spoken a parable, in other words, a metaphor. But they do not know *what* this one is a metaphor for. For Jesus has not said that this was to be a metaphor, has not said that *such-and-such is like* a sower who goes out to sow. Neither the crowds who have gone home nor the disciples understand what the metaphor means, nor why it is used; but at least the disciples know it is a metaphor and that something is being said other than an elementary lesson in agriculture. The crowds apparently do not even realize that. For them a literal statement has been made which is both true as far as it goes and insignificant. "I use parables when I speak to them because they look but do not see, they listen but do not hear or understand" (13:13). What they do not see or hear is that something about sowers and seeds will help them to think about something else by giving them a pattern or paradigm in which to think. That, of course, is the whole purpose of metaphor.

Jesus, then, is not speaking in riddles for the purpose of confusing his audience, as some have claimed. He is speaking metaphor for the purpose of helping them think. If they do not even see that his images are signals of something else, then of course they will take them as riddles and as nonsense, little bits of information that lead nowhere. That is their privilege. But Jesus is operating on a different basis from theirs. He assumes that, for the person who is thinking, for the person who is trying to figure things out, *everything is potentially a metaphor. Anything* might help such persons to think through their problems, whatever they are. The person whose mind is alive is looking all the time for comparison, so that nothing seen, not even the things most apparently irrelevant to and remote from his or her more immediate concerns, is ever merely dismissed.

A sower goes out to sow? Perhaps something *there* will help me think out my problem.

Two roads diverge in a yellow wood? If I am Robert Frost thinking about the decisions I have made, something about the two roads may help me to think about them.

Clocks and gears? If I am Isaac Newton, thinking about the movement of sun and planes, something about clocks might help my thinking along, might free me to think more clearly about those deeper things.

The thinking person is the one who has a problem but who is free to be surprised by a new metaphor into a viewpoint he or she never had before. For the person who is trying to figure out something, the world is full of metaphors. For the person who is not, it is full only of literal facts. Jesus reflects on sowers and seeds because something in them might open up an insight for him into whatever he happens to be thinking about; but the crowds hear about sowers and seeds and wonder why they should be wondering about sowers and seeds. Since they are not thinking about anything, no metaphor can help them to think.

The disciples, on the other hand, *are* thinking and *do* know that Jesus is using a metaphor. After he explains the matter, they also know *why* he uses one. But they still do not know just *what* is here being compared to sowers and to seeds. So they ask him point blank. Almost all scripture scholars agree that the explanation of the parable that follows was put on the lips of Jesus much later by members of the Christian community. They took the metaphor as they had received it from Jesus and operated on the assumption that something in it would help them to understand a problem that was bothering them at the time, a problem which may or may not have been quite like the one on Jesus' mind when he spoke his little treatise on the fate of seeds. The problem for the later believers seems to have been that a lot of the converts to Christianity were leaving their new faith. How could that be? Is God's word not powerful enough? Is there something wrong with this religion, that it cannot hold the people who are attracted to it? But if God's word is like the seed, and if the different people who hear it are like different kinds of ground.... The metaphor has saved the honor of God and the self-respect of the Christian faith. It has also put the apostates in their place. Whether this is exactly what Jesus meant no one will ever know, but his later followers did what the crowd on the shore did not do. They took what they knew to be a metaphor and made it work for them.

The same thing happens again with the next metaphor Jesus proposes, about wheat and weeds (13:24-30). He gives three more very short parables after that (13:31-35), and then the disciples ask for an application of the earlier one (13:36-43). It is applied to much the same effect as the parable of the sower who went out to sow. Evidently these two agricultural metaphors appealed in a particularly keen way to the imagination of the first generation of Jesus' followers, giving them meaningful terms in which to think out for themselves the solutions to the problems they were facing. It seems the other metaphors in this series of passages spoke to them less immediately, and they therefore felt perfectly free to pass them on without comment to the future generations who could use the metaphors in new ways for their own purposes.

The first parable in this set of passages, that of the sower, is not presented as a metaphor *of anything*. It is just presented, unapplied. All the others, however—the second parable of seeds (13:24-30), the mustard seed (13:31-32), the yeast (13:33), the hidden treasure (13:44), the pearl (13:45), the net (13:47-50), and the householder (13:52)—are explicitly presented as metaphors for "the kingdom of heaven," which, of course, is itself a metaphor. *Kingdom* was one of the favorite analogies of the Old Testament for defining the system of life under God. God was the King, the earthly king was his vice-regent who made the divine kingship tangible in the political life of the nation. The kingship of God was a system of authority and power, with emphasis on God's autocracy. It occupies in the Old Testament the same place Jesus' metaphor of fatherhood and sonship does in the New, that is, it is the main image in which is implied a whole way of life. By shifting the terms of the metaphor from *king* to *father,* and from *ruled* to *son,* Jesus clearly is trying to reinterpret the old images in a liberating sense. For too long they had been taken oppressively, implying a similarity between God and oriental potentates, to the detriment of God's goodness. Jesus uses a simple strategy to undo the mischief. He takes the old metaphor of kingship and allows himself the freedom to recast it in new metaphors taken from the life-giving world of nature, rather than from the death-dealing world of politics. Jesus takes the old metaphor and does startling things with it. Even though it has been hallowed by long use and authoritatively interpreted by a long line of serious people, he takes it as something no one has ever really thought about before. The received, authoritative, public wisdom is to be reconsidered and reinterpreted in the light of—of what? In the light of one's own fresh, personal metaphors; in the light of what this old thing feels like to this new man. Not one of these new metaphors for the Kingdom can be found in the Old Testament. They come, then, entirely from the imagination of Jesus, thinking and rethinking the notion of the "kingdom," walking about in his own world of farmers and grain, trees and birds, housewives and bread, merchants and pearls, fishermen and nets.

Your Turn   Jesus creates a wide variety of images for the kingdom. He does not pretend that any of them is saying everything there is to say on the subject; nor does he try to combine them all with each other to approximate a systematic idea of the nature of the kingdom. He is satisfied with glimpses of one aspect of the kingdom after another, and with insights that are not final. Thus:

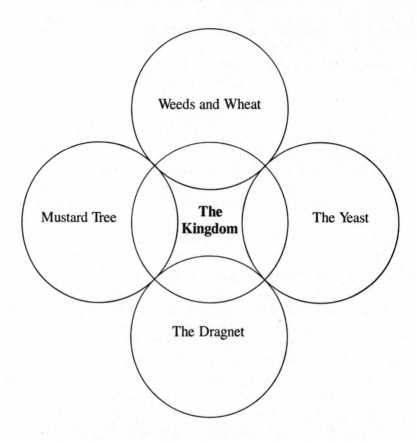

These metaphors do have something in common, though. They all describe the kingdom as a dynamic process rather than as a static hierarchy. Each metaphor describes a different sort of process, but they describe the processes according to the simple sequence of their beginning, middle, and end. The weeds and wheat are planted, mature, are cut down. And so on.

We invite the reader to do his or her own analysis of the four kingdom metaphors mentioned above by filling in the following charts. Across the top are questions designed to focus attention on the process of each direct analogy as it unfolds.

	Question 1: What does each parable say about the way the kingdom *begins?*	**Question 2:** What does each parable say about the way the kingdom *grows* or *develops?*
Weeds and Wheat		
Mustard Tree		
The Yeast		
The Dragnet		

	Question 3: What does each parable say about the way the kingdom comes to its *completion* or *fullness?*	**Question 4:** The four parables taken together seem to present the kingdom in paradoxically different attitudes toward those who might become its members. In each parable is the kingdom pictured as *generous* and *universal* and therefore open to all, or is it pictured as *judgmental* and *selective* and therefore not open to all?
Weeds and Wheat		
Mustard Tree		
The Yeast		
The Dragnet		

If you glance over the chart you will see that each direct analogy emphasizes something different about the kingdom. What part of the process does such direct analogy emphasize most?

Weeds and Wheat:

Mustard Tree:

The Yeast:

The Dragnet:

What does each one say about that part of the process?

Weeds and Wheat:

Mustard Tree:

The Yeast:

The Dragnet:

Compare your responses to someone else's to see how the same metaphor can evoke different responses.

Jesus, besides illustrating something about the kingdom of heaven here, is also showing something about the metaphorical way of thinking. One begins by having a specific concern—for Jesus it is the kingdom—and proceeds by actively looking for a very wide range of possible analogies, unwilling to settle too soon on any one image for fear of giving up too many of the nuances of the idea. Any idea worth thinking about is worth not being too definite about. Allowing and encouraging a wide range of analogies is a way of celebrating the richness of the idea.

The following exercise builds on the example of Jesus and is suggested as a way of helping you to explore your own way of doing metaphor.

For the next twenty-four hours, deliberately find as many direct analogies as you can to some idea that concerns you. Go through your normal occupations, but keep an eye open to possible analogies. We will mention a few possible topics to get you started, but invite you to think of your own if you can. Possible ideas would include: What is great *leadership?* What is *justice?* What is *will power?* Decide on one idea and write it down in the space below.

For the next twenty-four hours carry a pad and pencil with you and jot down anything that for any reason is analogous to your idea and that helps you to think about any aspect of it. Write each one down and state explicitly what the connection to the original idea is.

Direct Analogy   Connection

Again, compare your responses to someone else's. Or better, repeat the exercise with someone else on a topic you agree on. See how differently you respond to it.

Which of the new metaphors helped you to think in a new way about the topic? Those are the ones that exemplify best the purpose of metaphorical thought as used by Jesus in his re-examination of the old kingdom idea.

In fact, you might end this exercise by joining with Jesus in his exploration of the kingdom idea. Write your own parable, one that comes out of your own experience and imagination. If you wish a guideline for your parable, try using the dynamic process we describe in the chart given above. How does it begin, grow and develop? How does it come to a kind of completion? What does your metaphor suggest about membership in the kingdom?

The Kingdom of Heaven is Like....

Compare your parable to those written by others. Discover the different ways people have of making connections. Making metaphors opens the way to richer communication with others, as Jesus well knew.

All of the kingdom analogies we have explored so far deal with the kingdom as a dynamic process. Jesus uses another kind of metaphor that is much more static in a way, but much more suggestive about another aspect of the kingdom—why people seek it. He compares the kingdom to a treasure and to a pearl, two things that just sit there and do not seem to do much, and yet people will go to great lengths to possess them. The images of treasure and pearl suggest that the kingdom is *valuable,* and that it will be owned by people who can *recognize* a valuable thing when they see it.

He points out two kinds of people who find the kingdom. One deliberately sets out to find it, like the person in search of pearls. Another accidentally stumbles on to it, like the person who trips over a hidden treasure. Both ways work—provided that the person is capable of recognizing a value when he or she sees it. If the person cannot, no amount of search and no amount of luck will pay off. It is as Pasteur said: "Fortune favors the prepared mind."

The question, then, is: What kind of value does one have to recognize in order to perceive the kingdom when one is in its presence? Jesus offers the image of the hidden treasure and of the pearl to suggest an answer. Interestingly, he does not define what the treasure is. We are free to imagine a chest full of gold and diamonds if we are inclined that way. We are equally free to imagine another kind of treasure—say, a spectacular view or an abundance of precious wildlife. Jesus' first image leaves the kingdom's specific kind of value undefined, beyond simply that it is a "treasure."

His second image of the pearl goes further. The pearl has a particular kind of value. It is interesting that Jesus chose a pearl here because, while it may be quite expensive, it is certainly far from being the most lavishly expensive of the precious jewels in purely monetary terms. And it is an oddity from another point of view as well: among the jewels it alone is not brought to perfection by the work of a human craftsman.

And it is even a greater oddity from another point of view. It alone among the precious jewels is not a "rock," but was once part of a living system. And indeed, reflection shows that *all* of Jesus' analogies for the kingdom are taken from the domain of living things or (like yeast and wine) from among things intimately connected with life. Between the kingdom and nonliving things he seems to find no analogies. It seems therefore that if the kingdom is to be compared to a jewel at all, an inner necessity forces the choice of the pearl; no matter that it is not the most expensive bauble of them all. It has a special kind of—to return to the word—*value*.

Two things make a pearl utterly unique among jewels: the way it is formed, and the way it deals with the light passing through it. We will consider both things in an effort to explore Jesus' highly evocative metaphor of the kingdom.

How is a pearl formed? A grain of sand enters deep into an oyster, causing what must be very considerable discomfort. The oyster reacts by covering the grain with a secretion which normally would become part of its own inner shell. Layer after layer is secreted, and the pearl grows larger with each layer. It must cause a new kind of discomfort, for it is occupying the same tightly limited space as the oyster itself. All of this, by the way, takes place in total darkness. Only when the oyster is opened from outside does the pearl contact the light.

If you will re-read the previous paragraph you will see how oddly the process mimics sexual reproduction—and how completely different it is at the same time. Work out the points of comparison here:

Forming the Pearl	=	Sexual Reproduction

oyster   =   _____
                      because

grain of sand   =   _____
                      because

growth of pearl   =   _____
                      because

bringing pearl   =   _____
to light   because

In some fashion we have a "mother" (we even speak of "mother of pearl"), a "father," an "offspring," a "birth." But the analogy is highly misleading. Sexual reproduction would not make a pearl—it would make another oyster! If reproduction is being imitated here, it is also in a sense being parodied. At the least, the product of the asexual production is infinitely more valuable than the product of sexual reproduction would be— more valuable, that is, to someone other than the oyster. The oyster would prefer to have nothing to do with the pearl.

Find, then, major contrasts between the two systems. In the blanks write in the same items you mentioned above, but this time to highlight the contrasts.

Forming the Pearl	≠	Sexual Reproduction
oyster	≠	_____ because
grain of sand	≠	_____ because
the pearl	≠	_____ because
bringing pearl to light	≠	_____ because

We have here a kind of "fertility" or "generativity" fundamentally different from what we normally think of when we use those words. The really important thing about the analogy to sexual reproduction, therefore, is that it totally misrepresents what is really going on. It contributes nothing but error, and should be thrown out altogether.

Still, there is a "gestation" and "birth" going on here that strangely parallels the kind that Matthew paid so much attention to in the genealogies at the beginning of his gospel. If, for a moment, we take Jesus himself as "the pearl"—the offspring of great price—what has produced him?

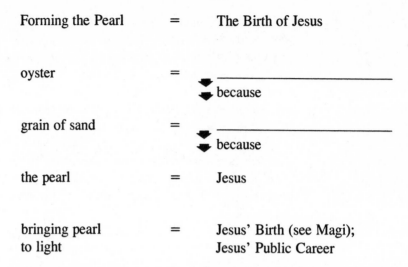

Forming the Pearl	=	The Birth of Jesus

oyster   =   _____
                       ↓ because

grain of sand   =   _____
                       ↓ because

the pearl   =   Jesus

bringing pearl   =   Jesus' Birth (see Magi);
to light   Jesus' Public Career

No doubt there are several possible ways of filling out the list, but we believe they all come down to the same thing. An obvious analogue to the oyster is the figure of Mary in the Virgin Birth; in this case, the equivalent of the sand implied in Matthew's text would be the "Spirit." But another analogue to the grain of sand—the "masculine" principle in this process—is the father himself, in which case the equivalent of the oyster—or the "feminine" principle here, or "matrix"—would be the Old Testament itself as embodied in the Jewish nation. If we line up these new analogies we have this:

1.		**2.**		**3.**
oyster	=	Old Testament	=	Mary
sand	=	Father	=	Spirit
pearl	=	Jesus	=	Jesus

The third column is a representation of the Virgin Birth, and a summary of the first chapter (on the genealogies) of this book. The second column is a representation of the central metaphor of Jesus' life and of Matthew's gospel, as well as a summary of the second chapter (on the baptism and temptations) of this book.

It should be noted that Christian symbolism for centuries has tended to see in Mary the embodiment of Israel and the culmination of the Old Testament. This fact tends to confirm that the implicit analogies being drawn out here are far from arbitrary; indeed, they seem to follow from an inner necessity which guided the choice of the pearl metaphor in the first place.

But what of this odd equation: sand = Father = Spirit? We have seen that the direct analogy of "father" for God has created as many problems as it solved. Its too exclusively masculine quality, its troublesome implications of generational conflict so common in family experience, the ambiguity of the kind of power fathers have and the kind of powerlessness sons have, all have made the notion of God as father difficult. Our analysis of the pearl, which implicitly lines up *father* with *spirit*, very strongly suggests that that metaphor of fatherhood which governs the universe of the gospel has to be taken in a highly qualified sense. It can be—has to be—denied as much as affirmed. Indeed, to refer to one and the same event as simultaneously the work of "father" and the work of "spirit" severely reduces the vividness of the paternal metaphor. It is even hard to see what is left of it. *Father* is full of sexual overtones; *Spirit* has none at all. The gospel, like most religious documents, has a strong masculine bias. It reflects the thought of its time. But in this parable there seems implied a broader viewpoint that breaks out of and transcends the traditional dominance of masculine energy.

Thus, the parable of the pearl suggests a different kind of metaphor for God—Spirit—and thereby is a correction of the central metaphor of Jesus' life and of Matthew's gospel, as well as a preview and a summary of the closing chapter of this book.

But all of this is implicit in the metaphor of the pearl, as it also is in the gospel of Matthew until the very end.

The formation of the pearl is one thing that makes it unique among jewels. The way it processes light is another. We have explored the first by "force fitting" the pearl's formation onto the main topic of the gospel. We will explore the second by means of personal analogy.

Unlike diamonds and all other crystals, the pearl does not allow light through itself in a simple fashion nor reflect it directly back in a single piercing flash. The pearl was built up layer by layer, and consequently its structure is that of many concentric spheres—the center itself being the original irritant, the bit of sand. As it enters the first layer, the light bounces around within that layer as well as being partially reflected outward again to the air and partially downward to the next layer.

The process is repeated in the next layer and the next, and so on until the light may be said to have filled the pearl completely. When the light reemerges it does not come out in very narrow "beams" as it would from a diamond. It comes out from every point on the pearl's surface. It is radiated rather than reflected.

Somehow, for Jesus the kingdom of heaven is "like" that. In that kind of behavior and way of being is its value. To explore how that might be so, we invite you to do a personal analogy fantasy on the pearl. By this time you have had considerable guided experience with this form of metaphor. We suggest that now you do it almost completely on your own.

We make only two suggestions to help focus the exercise. First, do it in two parts: when the pearl is in darkness within the oyster, and when the pearl is first exposed to the light. Secondly, address yourself to the question: What do the light and I contribute to each other—of what *value* are we to each other? Become that pearl before and after it is exposed to the light of the sun. What do you think and feel? Continue the exercise on your own.

Now *you* decide the issue. Just what do you think Jesus meant when he said the kingdom was like the pearl? Here is an opportunity for you to do with the pearl metaphor what the early Christians did with the parable of the sower, namely, to interpret it in the light of your own experience.

The kingdom parables show Jesus at his most poetic and playful. They also show him at his most purposeful, as a man thinking and rethinking one central set of concerns, at once very ancient and completely fresh.

Almost all his new metaphors correct some overemphasis or heaviness in the old images of the kingdom. The ponderous old kingdom is likened to the tiniest of all seeds, and the formalized and ritualized old kingdom is likened to a tree full of chirping birds (13:31-32). The massively solid old kingdom is transformed in Jesus' imagination into the fluffy and airy texture of a loaf of leavened bread (13:33). The oppressively *present* kingdom, altogether too visible everywhere in laws and customs, phylacteries and tassels, temple and synagogue, becomes in Jesus' mind something hidden and hard to see, never found on the surface, worth looking for behind the obvious (13:44-46).

But we know from earlier parts of Matthew's gospel that Jesus' vision cannot remain so uncomplicated for long. In the last parable in this section, that of the net (13:47-50), the bright new metaphor shows its darker side. The narrow and exclusive old kingdom is likened to a "dragnet thrown into a lake, which collected all sorts of things." It looks as though the walls of the kingdom, designed to keep other people out, are changed here to nets designed to bring them in. But that is not the sense of the thing as Jesus interprets it. For the net is not thrown by one interested in the superabundant variety of life in the sea; it is thrown by God's angels who want only a certain kind of fish and who will regard the rest as "useless" and to be thrown away. The old metaphor sneaks back into the new, and transforms the new meaning back into the old one, the liberating meaning back into the confining one. The same thing happened in the two parables of the seeds studied above. The old regal image of the kingdom is made homely and the old indoors-magisterial image is brought outdoors and made agricultural in the twin parables of farmers sowing seeds. But the first parable ends with most of the seeds parched and dead, the second ends with at least half the harvest in flames.

The new and old senses of the kingdom metaphor are both there. Now one may be dominant, and now another, but they are both always there. Jesus apparently cannot let go of either and prefers, even though they cannot logically be reconciled, to live with the real tension between them rather than to choose arbitrarily between them. It is a generous, if exceedingly difficult, way to live. He seems pleased enough with the approach to offer a metaphor for himself, as "the head of a household who can bring from his storeroom both the new and the old" (13:52).

Others Make Metaphors for Jesus

In the second set of passages under present consideration (13:53–16:20), it is not Jesus' sense of metaphor that is featured, but everyone else's. He is himself what everybody is thinking about, and is consequently the object rather than the source of metaphor. Everyone is trying to figure him out by determining what, exactly, to compare him to. They will display the same polarity between liberating and confining uses of metaphor that Jesus himself has just displayed.

There are essentially four groups of people in these passages, characterized by their four distinct ways of metaphorizing Jesus. The four groups are intermixed in the sequence of texts, but for analytical purposes we can sort them out and treat them separately. They are: (1) the people and the tetrarch Herod; (2) the Pharisees; (3) the sick and hungry; (4) the disciples. The four groups are arranged in order of increasing comprehension of what Jesus is all about, as evidenced by what they compare him to. (See Table I.)

Table I   Four Reactions to Jesus

	A. These people **Assimilate** a new experience to an old idea **Egocentrically**	**B.** These people **Assimilate** a new experience to an old idea **Ethnocentrically**	**C.** These people **Accommodate** an old idea to a new experience **Ethnocentrically**	**D.** These people **Accommodate** an old idea to a new experience neither **Egocentrically** nor **Ethnocentrically**
1	Jesus' relatives (13:53-58)			
2	Herod (14:1-12)			
3			Jesus feeds people (14:13-21)	
4	disciples at sea (14:22-27)	— — — — — to — — — — —		Peter at sea (14:28-33)
5			the sick (14:34)	
6		Pharisees and tradition (15:1-20)		
7			Canaanite woman (15:21-18)	
8			healings and second feeding (15:29-39)	
9		Pharisees and signs of times (16:1-4)		
10	disciples not understanding bread/yeast (16:5-12)	— — — — — to — — — — —		disciples understanding (16:12)
11				Peter's confession (16:13-20)

The People and the King

The first group consists of the unlikely combination of the people and the tetrarch Herod. They both exemplify a kind of thinking which is radically incapable of accepting anything new, so caught up is it in its own old and familiar thoughts. Anything new must be interpreted as being somehow just another example of what has been known all along. The new is both compared to and reduced to the old. Old experiences and reference points become the sole authoritative metaphor by which all other things will be measured. By the people Jesus is compared to—and reduced to—the people! They are the norm; if he is off the norm, that must be because he is abnormal, not because he may be exploring other and perhaps better norms. Here as always the thinking is accomplished by means of metaphor, but what shows up vividly is the metaphor's ability to serve neurosis as well as health; moral timidity and intellectual bankruptcy as well as vitality. That is what happens whenever the living and the new are compared to and reduced to the exhausted. Caught in their own clichés, the people cannot think of Jesus in any other terms than the ones they use for everything.

Perhaps this kind of pathology is even clearer in Herod. With absolutely no hesitation, Herod identifies Jesus as John the Baptizer raised from the dead (14:2). Jesus is not seen as Jesus, but is absorbed into Herod's obsession about John. John has a double hold on Herod's conscience, once because he had revealed the sin in Herod's marriage (14:4), and once again because Herod has had him murdered (14:10). John had challenged the moral and even the legal legitimacy of the tetrarch's reign; he had struck him where every king fears to be struck. Basing himself on his fears in much the same way that the people had based themselves on their habits, Herod thus compares Jesus to *and reduces him to* John, thus not recognizing him at all. Metaphors which are not acknowledged as such, and which therefore assume an increasingly dogmatic character and are enforced either by social convention or by personal neurosis, can have only one effect. They can only block off even the possibility of a fresh experience or a refreshed wisdom. They can only make everything new in the world seem as stale as they are themselves.

Pharisees and Sadducees

The second group who is trying to interpret Jesus by comparing him to something consist of the Pharisees and Sadducees. Clearly they are neither as provincial as the crowds nor as pathological as Herod, and yet they seem almost as totally incapable of comprehending him as the others were. Unlike the former groups, these more sophisticated and far less egocentric people have committed themselves to the tradition received from Moses and elaborated through the centuries by many holy people. The whole effort of such dedicated people is, indeed, to go beyond a narrow and obsessive egotism and into a wisdom both broad and deep, a way of life that puts one in continuity with the ages and with the God of the ages. In its anxiety to put the Pharisees in a bad light because of their rejection of Jesus, the New Testament invariably fails to give them credit for the selflessness of their dedication and for the sincerity with which they tried to go beyond personal prejudice and achieve something of God's own point of view. Unfortunately they walked into a trap, as do many people who have a single great dominating idea. For them—and in this they are like the crowds and Herod—anything which cannot be compared to their idea cannot be true. For example, there is only one way of observing the Sabbath; all alternatives are simply breaches of the Sabbath. If the behavior of Jesus and his disciples cannot be compared to the "tradition of our ancestors" (15:2), then it is not valid behavior, and that is all there is to be said about it. Once again a metaphor dictates in advance what shall or shall not be.

The Pharisees and Sadducees even come to Jesus on one occasion (16:1-4) to ask him for "some sign in the sky." They are not asking for a dazzling display of miracles, as Jesus clearly understands. As he explains, and they apparently agree, they are asking for something like a clue to the weather. If one wants to know the weather he should look at the sky for his clues. Likewise if he wants to understand Jesus, he should look at "heaven," that is, the realm of the divine, for his clues. The Pharisees, then, are asking Jesus to point to something—anything—in God's world to which he can be compared and by which they might be able to understand him. Clearly, all the comparisons the Pharisees have made of Jesus to the tradition have worked against him. So now they ask *him* to point up the sanctioned and received metaphor within the old tradition by which they might understand him. He points to "the sign of Jonah." That is, indeed, an image from the Hebrew Bible, and is in that sense a "sign from heaven." To that extent Jesus has complied with the request. But all he has done is highlight the total gulf between himself and the Pharisees. They can both use the same images but will never mean the same thing by them. As Jesus pulls the old metaphors into new senses the Pharisees pull them back to their classical sense, and there the communication ends, at the very point where it begins.

The Hungry and the Sick

The third group of people who try to understand Jesus by comparing him to something are the hungry and the sick. The hungry implicitly compare him to Moses; the sick compare him to the messianic figure who appears at the end of the Book of Isaiah. Jesus is to the people's hunger in Palestine as Moses was to the people's hunger in the desert. The sight of the bread triggers a memory of the manna, and the connection between Jesus and Moses is confirmed (see Ex. 16). Unlike the Pharisees and Sadducees, then, the hungry people do find "a sign from heaven"; that is, they find something within their people's history with God to which Jesus can be compared. Similarly, the sick who come to him for healing do so with the memory fresh in their minds of the strange messianic person presented in Isaiah (Isa. 65:1ff), the same figure to whom also Jesus has already compared himself (Mt. 11:4-6). The hungry and the sick, then, behave similarly to the other two groups we have considered insofar as they too look to the past to find a point of comparison for Jesus. But for the first two groups, the metaphor from the past was the norm to which anything in the present had to conform, whereas for the present group the images and patterns that have come down from the past are a *preparation* for understanding something present. What these people already know from their religious tradition is not the last word, but can be used as a springboard toward a new insight. It can be interpreted in a progressive sense. Past knowledge for them is not the whole of all possible knowledge. It is still open to new interpretations and applications. Metaphors drawn from the past help to shed light on the only thing that really exists, namely, the present. For these people, the interaction between themselves and Jesus is the primary reality, to be reflected upon with the help of analogies from the past. For the other groups we have considered, precisely the opposite was true. The present was allowed to exist only to the extent that it conformed to patterns already laid down once and for all. The crucial difference lies in the way earlier knowledge and experience are used when one is confronted with something new. Does one *reduce* the new to the old as the people and the tetrarch Herod did? Does one *deny* the new to defend the old as the Pharisees did? Or does one *adapt* the old as a rough, fair sketch of the new as the hungry and the sick did? Those are three ways of using a metaphor, two to prevent and one to open up the possibility of a broadened and deepened world.

The Disciples

There is still another way of using metaphor, as exemplified by still another group of people in these passages. The group consists of Jesus' disciples. The reader is referred again to Table I. This group is especially interesting because it is the only one which changes columns on this grid. In other words the disciples at first tend to show roughly the same characteristics as the people and Herod, but they do a radical about-face afterwards. In one passage (14:22), they are endangered at sea. Jesus is said to appear to them in these dreadful circumstances, and the disciples react— quite automatically and unconsciously— by comparing this present apparition to something archaic in their imaginations: "It is a ghost!" (14:26). Herod had had much the same reaction.

In another passage (16:5) something less dramatic but still quite revealing happens. Jesus warns the disciples to beware of "the yeast of the Pharisees."

The disciples are puzzled by this remark, taking it as they do altogether literally. Leaven is leaven. This is very much like the reaction of the people. Jesus upbraids his disciples for their lapse into literalism—and for a very good reason: the literal person will never understand what Jesus is all about.

But in both instances, the disciples overcome their momentary regression, and in the person of Peter especially, they devise a new metaphor for Jesus. Unlike the Pharisees they do not take a strictly-interpreted metaphor from the tradition, and unlike the hungry and the sick they do not adapt any metaphors from the past to the present. They simply metaphorize Jesus the same way he metaphorizes himself: He is *the son*. The difference, then, between the sick or hungry and the disciples lies simply in whether one understands Jesus as Jesus understands himself. The sick and hungry are not disciples because, however sympathetic to Jesus and his message, however grateful for his power, they do not think in quite the same metaphors.

The four groups of people show that the controversy about how to understand Jesus is also, on a more abstract plane, a controversy about how to use metaphor in the task of understanding anything whatever. Metaphor frequently, operating on an unconscious level as for the first group, exercises a hidden control over one's thinking and leads to mere blindness. Sometimes it operates as for the second group: a pattern fully conscious and fully explicit to which everything *must* conform regardless of whether it *does* conform or not—reality may not be bigger than or other than the metaphor. Again, it can be the tool by which one gains a first grasp of new dimensions of experience, as it was for the third group, who were not afraid to use an old idea as a lead into a new one. And finally, metaphor can function as it does for the disciples and for Jesus himself, as the root statement of a new view of the universe.

John the Baptizer and Satan, absent now for many chapters in their own persons, are still present in the dilemma they were the first to expose in Jesus' new way of living. It was the dilemma of whether to take the new metaphor of father and son—and also the old metaphor of king and subjects—in a liberating or a confining sense. Jesus lives out the dilemma, experiencing both of its poles. He finds no solution to it, and perhaps the *really* new thing about him is that, unlike either John or Satan, and unlike the other figures we have considered in the present chapter, he settles for no solution at all. He settles for the paradox itself, as being at least more real than settling for only one side of it.

Father and Son:
Exploring the Metaphor

6. Old vs. New: Conflicts in the Image of the Temple

(Matthew 16:21—26:25)

The last chapter studied Jesus' use of metaphor to gain new personal insights into the idea of God's "kingdom." It also studied the ways various groups of people use metaphor to gain an insight into Jesus himself. The present chapter is a study of Jesus' attempt to come to terms with the leading metaphor of the world into which he was born.

John and Satan had posed one version of the dilemma Jesus had to face. Satan and the Pharisees posed a second version. For the Pharisees there were traditionally-sanctioned ways of thinking, and the sanction of tradition was necessary if the thinking was to be considered valid. Satan emphasized instead being confident in one's own viewpoint, finding the sanctions for one's thoughts in one's own self and in one's own experience. Just as he had to live out the first version of the dilemma, so Jesus will have to live out the second.

Robert Frost speaks of those "metaphors that do our thinking for us"—those patterns of thought transmitted by the culture and sanctioned by long use, which have the advantage of helping us to think at all and the disadvantage of making us think only one way. Much of people's efforts to think for themselves lies in their effort to figure out what attitude to take toward those great received metaphors which sum up the wisdom of the past and come ready-made for use as the wisdom of the present and the future as well. Does one *replace* them? *reject* them without replacing them? accept them while *changing* them? *accept* them without changing them? Those seem to be the alternatives. Any thinking which takes place in the context of an on-going tradition—and that is *all* thinking—can be characterized in one of those four ways.

Sometimes, as in the case of Jesus in the passages under consideration in the present chapter, the thinking has to be characterized in all four ways—now one way, now another, and another, and another. It gives some sense of the magnitude of Jesus' effort to define himself and redefine the world he inherited to see him try out every strategy the human mind has for the task.

The intensity of his effort and the variety of his approaches to it can be seen most graphically in what seems to be the strangest argument of his life, his argument with a piece of architecture in the center of Jerusalem. In the series of passages presently under study, Jesus exhibits toward the Temple all four of the approaches just mentioned, apparently unconcerned about contradicting himself, because he was more concerned with exploring his relationship to the Temple from all possible angles. His earliest attitude toward the Temple as recorded by Matthew is, simply, to accept it, to go along with it and its customs and laws. Other gospels are more explicit, showing Jesus going to the Temple for worship on various occasions. But Matthew simply relates an exchange between Peter and Jesus about the tax required by the Book of Exodus for the "tent of meeting," the forerunner of the later Temple built by King Solomon, destroyed by Babylonian invaders, and rebuilt by Herod the Great. In Jesus' day as in Moses', the tax was for the support of the nation's main—indeed, only—sanctuary. Jesus asks Peter rhetorically whether, as free sons rather than captives or slaves, they should be forced to pay the tax—it is a question asked by all tax-payers—but concedes it is not worth making a fuss about it. He tells Peter to pay the tax for both of them, getting the money out of the mouth of the first fish he catches from the sea (17:24-27). This charming episode shows Jesus and Peter to be privately a touch irreverent about the Temple and its ways, but still recognizing the authority of the institution and willing to go according to its requirements. Jesus, whose opposition to the main religious sects of his day has already grown to very large proportions, nevertheless accepts for himself the Temple's prescriptions as he had also earlier urged them on the two lepers he cured. Just as he was to pay the tax, they were to show themselves to the priest (8:4). For Jesus the Temple was a fact of life and its laws and ways were part of the structure of life.

Or, more accurately, that is one of several attitudes he had toward it. A less placid feeling shows up in the remarkably violent scene in which Jesus enters the Temple to drive out the money-changers and peddlers of various religious items (21:12-17). He does this, not at all as an attack on the Temple but in the name of what the Temple really ought to be—a house of prayer. His attitude here is more complex than in the episode of the tax payment, for here, while he does accept the validity of the Temple, he does not accept it *as it is*. It must first be *changed*, returned to its original ideal, before it can be accepted in fact as well as in principle. So Jesus tries on the attitude of a religious reformer, accepting the religious structure but in a different sense and with a different emphasis than was normal in his time. It is almost as if there are two temples, two structures, at war with each other.

But Jesus also assumes a third attitude, far more searing than the first two. Fully aware of his extremely dangerous position before the religious establishment, he *rejects* the Temple and, as he does so he says of it, "I assure you, not one stone will be left on another—it will all be torn down" (24:1-2). This is not a philosophical remark on how all things perish in due season. It is a mental assault by Jesus on the entire structure of the Temple, its laws, and its way of life, which, if the assault could ever be translated into physical and military terms, would be a total blitzkrieg. Now the structure is not merely being corrected but demolished, and with a vengeance. Now there is no more distinction between the Temple as it is and the Temple as it is supposed to be—there is just the Temple as such, and it is turned over in wish and in imagination to the sackers and despoilers. Now there is no hint of paying the tax, miraculous fish or no miraculous fish. The Temple from any point of view, from all points of view, has to die.

But even that does not exhaust the range of Jesus' attitudes toward this great building. There is still another attitude, a fourth, perhaps the strangest of all. Jesus goes the last full step and in his own mind sees himself as being a rival Temple to the one that stood at the center of Jerusalem. He sees himself as the *replacement* of the old Temple. The idea seems almost insane, and indeed when it is quoted at his trial by hostile witnesses, it does seem insane: "This man has declared, 'I can destroy God's sanctuary and rebuild it in three days' " (26:61). But the witnesses have shifted the meaning a bit and have, if anything, diminished the strangeness of the remark. They make it seem as though Jesus had delusions about his skills as an engineer and contractor, that he is a carpenter gone berserk, an architectural maniac. But the madness is quite different. The temple he refers to is not the Jewish Temple; it is he himself. The destruction and rebuilding is that of he himself. If his true meaning had been perceived at the trial, this one remark would have been the evidence that killed him. But he was incorrectly understood to be making a vicious but quite impossible guerrilla threat against a piece of holy real estate. Earlier on, Jesus had given clues of his meaning—as when he conducted his own ministry of healing within the very walls of the Temple, setting himself up as the Temple's competition (21:14)—but again the larger meaning had gone unnoticed. His enemies took offense at the lesser dimensions of what he did, not the larger. Even as his enemies close in for the kill, they still do not see how radical a thing has happened. In his own mind, Jesus has become the authentic Temple, replacing the inauthentic one; he is himself the structure within which the business between God and humanity henceforth will be conducted.

There can be little doubt that Jesus' attitudes toward the Temple and his relationship to it at one time or another can be characterized in all four ways described here. And there can be little doubt, too, that there is a lot of movement from being cooperative at the beginning of his career to being antithetical at the end. But it would not be enough to say that Jesus merely changes from being a friend to being a reformer, to being a foe, to being a replacement, or that there is a straight-line progression from his first position to his last. As his attitudes are discussed here, there is indeed a logical continuum from the first to the fourth attitude, but the logic is being superimposed on to the gospel portrait of Jesus. His several attitudes toward the Temple do not actually exist in a pure state, distinct from each other, following each other in right order. Rather, all four of them seem to exist simultaneously, now one dominant, now another, but all four present, all four possible, all active. The fact is, Jesus has several attitudes toward the Temple which are in a kind of competition among themselves as to which will be *the* attitude. If people were simply logical beings, this could never be the case; but since they are also psychological beings who work out their values and beliefs as much by feeling them as by thinking them, as much by acting as by arguing them, it *is* the case. It is sometimes called "ambivalence," but that word suggests a condition in which one has *two* conflicting attitudes toward the same thing as the same time; here is a situation in which there are four, and that is probably more normal than not in questions of great moment.

What is the strange business about between the man and the building? To answer the question, it is necessary to re-examine the Temple itself, not as an individual physical *building,* but as a *structure* at once physical and moral, a *context* within which certain kinds of deeds, thoughts, and affections are appropriate and others not. As a physical structure, this Temple, like any building, makes some movements possible and others not, encourages some and embarrasses others. Like any building, it pre-structures what those who enter it will do and will not do. It is not just a closing off of space; it is a closing off of human possibilities, a canceling of some in a celebration of others. The Temple, like any building, is the structure *outside* of a person which limits and channels one's movements.

But the Temple is not just any building. Besides being a physical structure, it is also the emblem and embodiment of a mental and moral one. Its significance for Jesus, as for his opponents, lies in its character as a metaphor in stone for the traditions of the culture which built it. It is when the Temple is understood to be a metaphor that its importance for Jesus can be understood. It is what all great metaphors are, a structuring principle of life, a summary of what life has felt like in the past, and a blueprint of what it shall and should feel like in the present and in the future. The Temple is, then, a metaphor of the same magnitude and order as Jesus' own, and its purpose is exactly the same. The two grand metaphors are trying to occupy the same ground at the same time, and that ground is the mind of Jesus. The tension within him, then, is of the kind that is possible only for a person who takes fully seriously both the great central metaphors which come from one's cultural tradition and those which come from one's own soul. The person for whom one of these is missing will never realize the enormity of what Jesus did when he allowed both of them into his mind and life.

Your Turn   Look back over the worlds you said you were part of in the exercise on the Beatitudes (page 75). What one literal, physical building stands for and is the context of each of those worlds (as, for example, your house is most likely the building that stands for and is the context of your family world)?

World	Building
1.	
2.	
3.	
4.	

These are your four "temples." Each one is a metaphorical structure that expresses you and your values, but that also to some extent fails to express you adequately and may even distort or contradict the way you see yourself.

Suppose you have the same four attitudes toward each of your "temples" that Jesus had toward his. On the following chart try to make them explicit. Let "1." stand for the first building, and in each column to the right of the number jot down how the attitude named above is true of you in relation to that structure. Do the same thing for each of the other three "temples."

	Accept as is	Change it	Reject it	Replace it
1.				
2.				
3.				
4.				

In each case circle the attitude you feel the most strongly identified with.

In each case draw jagged lines around the attitudes you feel most strongly negative about. (Nothing says, by the way, that they can't be the same!)

If you had only *one* attitude toward each building—the one you have circled—and if the other attitudes were not at all part of you, how would that change the way you behaved there?

1.

2.

3.

4.

If you had *only* the attitudes you drew jagged lines around?

1.

2.

3.

4.

If you had *only* the attitudes you neither circled nor drew jagged lines around?

1.

2.

3.

4.

The fact is that we, more often than not, have multiple attitudes toward the various dimensions of our lives. But few of us allow those attitudes such full expression as Jesus did.

The Temple is a massive external image of the inner, psychological structures that both express and constrict us. Jesus finally came to the position that the Temple would have to be destroyed before any new way of structuring one's life with the father-God would be possible. He came to exactly the same position regarding the psychological structures we all carry around with us. They, too, finally will have to be destroyed and transcended because, although they express a part of us, they also limit and even stifle our fuller selves. He said it this way: "If a man wishes to come after me, he must deny his very self, take up his cross, and begin to follow in my footsteps. Whoever would save his life will lose it, but whoever loses his life for my sake will find it. What profit would a man show if he were to gain the whole world and destroy himself in the process? What can a man offer in exchange for his very self? The Son of Man will come with his Father's glory accompanied by his angels.

When he does, he will repay each man according to his conduct" (16:24-27).

Everyone experiences a variety of moods, occupations, roles, and activities which, taken all together, make up what we usually think of as one's "identity." But these lesser selves—which Psychosynthesis calls sub-personalities—are so many metaphorical temples that both structure and stifle our deeper lives and our fuller and more central identity.

Who Are You?

Answer that question in at least twenty different specific ways. Begin each response with "I am...." For example, "I am the daughter of x and y." "I am a middle-management executive with an OK job and not much future." "I am a third-generation American citizen with Republican leanings."

Those are the twenty or so "you's," but none of them is the central You. Instead, they are each manifestations of a part of You which we are calling a sub-personality. Some of those twenty "you's" have things in common with each other, and so can be taken together as reflections or extensions of a *single* sub-personality, that is, a single cluster of feelings, thoughts, activities, even bodily aspects that *almost, but not quite* amount to a full personality.

For example, a person might identify several roles he or she plays: parent, spouse, church-goer, contributor to certain charities. All these roles might be seen as sharing characteristics of generosity, concern, empathy, quiet strength. But the same person might also identify other very different roles: gun-carrying police officer, strong political partisan, anti-smut organizer, supervisor at work. All these roles might be seen as sharing characteristics of authority, worry, competitiveness, combativeness. In these eight roles, then, we have really only two sub-personalities. A person who plays all these roles is acting out of two major identity structures within his or her overall personality.

Go back over the list of the twenty "you's" and pick out five sub-personalities. Look for significant things that a number of these roles have in common. Describe the characteristics that are peculiar to each sub-personality; give each sub-personality a name and write a description of it:

Sub-personality 1. (name) _____
               (description)

Sub-personality 2. (name) _____
               (description)

Sub-personality 3. (name) _____
               (description)

Sub-personality 4. (name) _____
               (description)

Sub-personality 5. (name) _____
               (description)

    This list may look like the descriptions of five different people. But to illustrate that they are all aspects of You, put the name of each sub-personality into one of the spaces in the "pie" diagram. Note that You are in the center as the point which coordinates these sub-personalities. Note, too, that in the diagram some sub-personalities would go well alongside of each other (almost as allies), while some belong opposite to each other (almost as antagonists). Fill out the diagram so as to bring out these relationships among the sub-personalities.

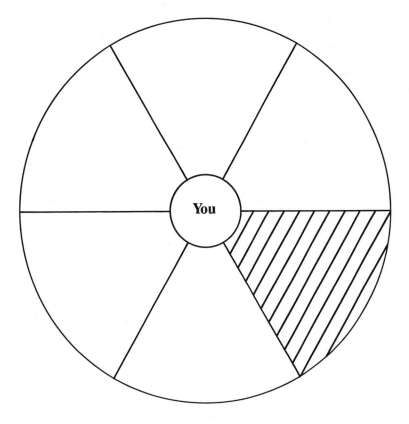

Leave one space free so that there will be room for that subjectivity that is yet to be discovered.

How is each of these sub-personalities related to that You in the center? To help you answer the question, write a brief dialogue between that central You and each sub-personality. Allow each sub-personality to begin the dialogue by saying what it wants and needs; then allow the center to answer. Imagine you are able to step into each section of the "pie" to begin the dialogue and to step back into the center to listen and respond. Be especially clear about the distinction between "I want" and "I need"—what "I want" is immediate and particular; what "I need" is larger and more permanent. For example, "I want" candy; but when I say that I may really mean that "I need" nourishment because I am hungry. Or, for that matter, I may mean that "I need" something to chew on to work off nervous energy because I am worried.

Response by the Central *You*

Sub-personality 1.

    I want

    I need

Sub-personality 2.

    I want

    I need

Sub-personality 3.

    I want

    I need

Sub-personality 4.

    I want

    I need

Sub-personality 5.

    I want

    I need

    Each of your sub-personalities has one kind of life, and the central You has quite a different, deeper kind. What is their relationship to each other? We have been stressing the dynamic and largely positive character of that relationship as a series of vital exchanges. But each sub-personality can also prevent one's reaching the fuller, deeper, and more coherent identity of the central self. The person who identifies himself or herself *too much* as an authority, or as a helper, or as an official, is simply failing to own the fullness of himself or herself. That is when the sub-personalities can and do become one's enemies.

Re-read the words of Jesus with which we began this part of the exercise (Matthew 16:24-27). "Losing" one kind of life in order to "gain" another and deeper kind may mean, then, ceasing to identify with any sub-personality and beginning to identify with the "You" at the center of them all. Answer for each of the sub-personalities you have distinguished what it would mean to "lose" it, that is, to stop identifying with it and to identify instead with the You at the center:

Sub-personality 1.

Sub-personality 2.

Sub-personality 3.

Sub-personality 4.

Sub-personality 5.

The Temple had become for many Jews a sort of sub-personality with which they identified too completely and too exclusively, to the detriment of other dimensions and possibilities in their life with God. It makes no difference whether a sub-personality expresses itself through the structure of a building or the structure of one's inner feeling and attitudes. It comes to the same thing—getting trapped in a metaphor that starts off by *expressing* a larger reality but that ends up *substituting* itself for it. At that point the friend has become the enemy. Jesus' argument with the building and his stress on the need to lose one's life mean the same thing: Get out of the trap.

A metaphor is a structure in which thought, feeling, or action takes place. In that fact lies the Temple's significance for Jesus. But his attempt to work out his relationship to that structure is not confined to the Temple itself. For the Temple is only one version of that structure. There are other, verbal versions of it which Jesus treats in exactly the same way as he does the Temple itself. There are great central images which structure life for him every bit as much as stone walls and open courts. For him and his people two of the greatest images were those of the covenant and the kingdom.

The covenant was really several covenants, one with Noah, another with Abraham, still another with Moses. *Covenant* means a legal contract, an exchange of binding promises, in this case between God and either a person or a people. *Covenant* was the oldest and most basic metaphor which structured life for the Jewish people.

A newer one was *kingdom*. It was essentially a variation on the first, but where *covenant* is a general legal term used in any kind of society, *kingdom* is more specific. It refers to a particular kind of society, in which power is centralized, consecrated, and applied. Power is the way of life. Thus, the making of the "covenant" was gradually reinterpreted as the establishment of a "kingdom"; that is, the exchange of promises gave God the people's obedience and gave the people the security of God's power. It was a subtle shift within the original idea. For *covenant* did not have to mean *kingdom*; it could also, and for some people did, mean *marriage*, so that God and Israel were seen as lovers and spouses. But the kingdom metaphor largely won out. The covenant, then, had to do with God's power and authority—and his ability to take revenge, that inevitable prerogative of kings.

The idea of the kingdom was a metaphor of a metaphor. By means of a second analogy the first analogy was further defined. In the last chapter attention was focused on Jesus' attempts to re-define the kingdom metaphor itself, by means of his own new analogies for it. What the attempt was for should be clearer now. If the idea of *kingdom* shifted the idea of *covenant* in the direction of power and politics, the idea of *leaven* or of *mustard seeds* or of *pearl* might shift it back again to something less political and static, more organic and fluid. Unfortunately this third range of metaphor—a metaphor of a metaphor of a metaphor—was not to be occupied by the kind of images Jesus offered for it. For the world around him had already settled on another third-order metaphor which further defined *kingdom,* which in turn had further defined *covenant.* The accepted third-order metaphor was *money,* or more particularly *payment of debts.* The payment was usually in money, though sometimes in one form of homage or other. But generally *money* and the *payment of debts* was the way the relationships of human beings to God and one person to another were envisioned within this kingdom-covenant. In a word, all other resonances of the word *covenant* were eliminated, and the word came to mean *contract* in the most exact fiscal sense. It is hard to think of this as anything but a deterioration in meaning. And yet these are the metaphors that defined the lives of so many of the people: *covenant* and *kingdom* and *debt.* These were the structure within which life was to be lived.

They were, in other words, equivalent to that other key metaphor, the Temple itself. It therefore could not be enough for Jesus to work out his relationship to the Temple by itself, unless the Temple was literally what he cared about. But his concern was with the whole way of structuring the life of human beings and God within his culture. What Jesus did with the Temple he had to do also with those other master metaphors of *covenant*, *kingdom* and *debt.* In the other passages under present consideration, that is exactly what he did, and it should come as no surprise that he had the same range of responses to these images as he had to the Temple itself. Does he *accept* them? accept but *change* them? *reject* them? reject and *replace* them? Once again the answer is yes to all possibilities.

Table II arranges the series of 36 passages in this section of the gospel schematically. From top to bottom they are arranged in the sequence in which they occur in the text. From left to right they are arranged according to which attitude of humanity on Jesus' part they seem to reflect: *replace* the old metaphor with a new one (A), *reject* the old (B), use the old but *change* it (C), simply *accept* the old (D). The passages already discussed concerning the Temple have been boxed for easy identification. It should also be noticed that of the 36 passages there are only eight—those in the first column—in which the old language of *covenant-kingdom-money* is simply replaced with something else. In the other passages the old language is used, but in a variety of ways. What the reader of these ten chapters of the gospel is witnessing, then, is a mind using every strategy at its command to rethink the very meaning of life.

Table II	A. Replace	B. Reject	C. Change	D. Accept
1				lose-save life 16:24-28
2	possessed son 17:14-21			
3				Temple tax 17:24-27
4	be like children 18:1-9			
5	stray sheep 18:10-14			
6	fraternal correction 18:15-18			
7	power of prayer 18:19-20			
8			king settles accounts 18:21-35	
9				against divorce 19:1-12
10	blesses children 19:13-15			
11		danger of riches 19:16-22		
12		eye of the needle 19:23-26		
13				hundredfold reward 19:27-30
14			laborers in vineyard 20:1-16	
15		mother of James & John 20:20-23		
16		authority = service 20:24-28		
17	cure of blind men 20:29-34			
18	curing in the Temple 21:14		cleansing of Temple 21:12-17	

Table II	A. Replace	B. Reject	C. Change	D. Accept
19				fig tree 21:18-22
20		rejects priests & elders 21:23-27		
21		two sons 21:28-32		
22				householder & tenants 21:33-41
23				cornerstone 21:42-43
24				wedding banquet 22:1-14
25		render to Caesar 22:15-22		
26		marriage & resurrection 22:23-33		
27	great commandment 22:34-40			
28		David & Lord 22:41-46		
29		Scribes & Pharisees Ch. 23		
30		destruction of Temple 24:1-3		
31				coming of Son of Man 24:4-51
32				ten virgins 25:1-13
33				talents 25:14-30
34				last judgment 25:31-46
35		anointing 26:6-13		
36		betrayal 26:14-16		

Note: Five passages in this section have been omitted from Table II. They will be discussed in the next chapter. They are:

The Transfiguration	17:1-13
Prediction of Passion	17:22-23
Prediction of Passion	20:17-19
Entry into Jerusalem	21:1-11
Prediction of Passion	26:1-5

No attempt will be made here to discuss each passage in detail. But each group of passages should receive comment in order to make clear how the battle of the metaphors was fought.

Column A

The texts in the first column make no use at all of the old vocabulary. They simply replace it. They use a new language based upon a new metaphor, that of filial and fraternal love under the fatherhood of God. These passages speak in the language and show the deeds of that vision with which Jesus began his public life. In these passages we are returned to the original freshness and simplicity of that exquisite vision, uncomplicated by darker considerations and free of old prejudices or ugly arguments. A man brings his sick, self-destructive boy to Jesus (17:14-18). Jesus restores the boy to his senses and to the boy's father. It is the very image of what had happened in Jesus' baptism, which was to be the first moment of a new filial and fraternal harmony under the fatherly God. In the other passages Jesus repeatedly urges people to see themselves only as children and brothers. He urges them not to despise children, but to see in them the image of what is best in human beings. Even if a child resembles a straying sheep sometimes—Jesus is realist enough to see the possibility (18:10-14)—still that is the image of what the father, here compared to a shepherd, loves. And if people are to be corrected for their straying ways, the correcting is to be done as among brothers, with kindness and patience, never with an intention to wound (18:15-18). The purpose is to restore vision to the blind (20:29-34)—above all, to restore to a blind world the vision of the two great commandments which are law enough for fathers and sons (22:34-40).

These passages contain what is most personal in Jesus' thoughts and least borrowed from any other source, although some of his words even here are straight from the Old Testament. Their serenity of tone is rare in the gospel, for Jesus is seldom free of the need to deal with other points of view than his own. Mainly, of course, he has to deal with the covenant-kingdom-payment point of view, that other version of the Temple point of view. It is important not to forget that this latter way of seeing things, though quite foreign to most people today, was the standard and universal wisdom of Jesus' day. It is the wisdom he was born into. It is the epitome of his entire culture. Thus, when we examine the way he relates to these inherited metaphors, we examine also the way he relates to the whole society and culture of which they are the wisdom.

Column B

Another of his characteristic responses to these images, as to the Temple, is a determined *rejection* of them. The passages listed in the second column are grouped together because in each of them some aspect of the conventional metaphor is being explicitly denied. The first three texts in the list constitute a small sermon warning against approaching life in money terms. Thinking money and thinking God at the same time is virtually impossible. Jesus gives no reason for this, but probably it is because the accumulation of wealth gives one the illusion of power and control, two attributes which for Jesus belong to God alone. For people to deal in money involves them, regardless of their best intentions, in setting up rival providences. It is not the attitude of the birds of the air or the lilies of the field. And so Jesus rejects the whole manner of thinking—until the last sentence of this small sermon (19:29), where he himself uses the money metaphor to speak of "inheriting" eternal life. Mainly he is rejecting the mode of thought connected with money, but he cannot completely avoid it himself. It is clear, though, especially in two of the most moving passages in the whole gospel—his anointing and his betrayal—that Jesus utterly rejects reducing life to a set of fiscal transactions. He praises the waste of money involved in the purchase of a luxurious ointment because the love expressed in the extravagance is far more important than the imprudence. To assert the claims of prudence would undo an act of love. And if the act of wasting money is a fitting sign of love for Jesus, the act of making money is a fitting emblem of his betrayal.

Prudent fiscal transactions, then, are what life in Jesus' world is *not* about. Nor is it about that other thing that underlies money, namely, the whole idea of owing anything, whether it be money or obedience or homage. For debts can be paid in more than coin. In other passages in this series Jesus rejects, in addition to money in a narrow sense, the whole system of authority and status that money makes possible. He rejects out of hand the mother's request that her sons be given places of honor and power in Jesus' kingdom. Jesus turns the idea around on her, says that in *his* kingdom—as against the kingdom this woman was thinking of—the only status belongs to those who serve others (20:20-28). In *his* kingdom the old contracts and the whole system of legalized transactions are gone, including after the final resurrection the contractual arrangement called marriage (22:23-33); in *his* kingdom the interrelationships of people are so thrown off their normal course that King David even calls one of his own descendants "Lord" (22:41-46), as egregious a reversal of the *right* way of doing things as was the purchase of the ointment.

Whether he talks of money transactions in the narrow sense or of legalized, contractualized human relations in a broader sense, Jesus in these passages is simply tearing up the system. A kingdom so overturned will be a political shambles; a covenant in which contracts are all canceled will be a jurisprudential ruin. Jesus nowhere rejects the triad of covenant-kingdom-money more eloquently than in his tirade against the Scribes and Pharisees (Chapter 23). The traffic in money and laws and status—even holy money, holy laws, and holy status—has no place in a world where "justice and mercy and good faith" (23:23) are what matter. Just as he threatened the destruction of the Temple, so Jesus threatens the demolition of a whole way of thinking about the life of human beings with God. His rejection of the old metaphor is complete.

Column C

Or so it would seem if it were not for other passages still to be considered. In the third column there are only two passages, but they—unlike the passages we have just examined—are so intricate in their handling of the classical metaphors that they reveal an entirely different dimension of Jesus' thinking. In these passages, as in the scene of the cleansing of the Temple, Jesus is taking the images in a double sense. In the cleansing of the Temple, he was accepting the Temple on one level but challenging and changing it on another. The same thing is happening in these other two passages with the metaphors of covenant, kingdom, and money.

The first passage (18:21-35) is the famous story of the merciful king and the unmerciful servant. All the classical images are there: the kingdom, the king, the status, the power, the settling of accounts, the servant, the debt, the failure of payments, the punishment. Jesus is picturing the relationship of human beings and God exactly according to the old ideas, even to the servant's fatuous plea for "patience." So far so good. The old metaphor is intact and unfolds as expected. But then the king himself steps out of character and not only does not take revenge, not only shows unexpected patience, but simply cancels the debt and thereby introduces an entirely new factor: mercy. Nothing in covenants, kings, or finances calls for that. The introduction of mercy and of the canceling of debts alters the transaction radically. But the servant then goes out and acts toward someone in his debt as the king should have acted toward him. The servant acts within and according to the old metaphors, whereas the king himself *changed* them—"cleansed" them, as it were, as Jesus has cleansed the Temple. It all seems a very straightforward critique of the old metaphors, which by contrast show up as poorly against the new as the cruel servant does against the merciful king.

But there is further complication. The failure of the servant to act in the new way forces the king to act again in the old way. The king reverts to type, and throws the servant in jail "till he should pay all his debt." He cancels the cancelation of the debt, and renews the whole ancient arrangement of things down to the last detail. It is a remarkable performance. The world of king, contract, and debt is both changed and confirmed. It is a schizophrenic world in which merciful kings still turn harsh and canceled debts are still remembered and the emptied prisons can still be filled again. Jesus is thinking two ways at once. He cleanses the Temple, but in the cleaning reestablishes its authority.

The other story—that of the laborers in the vineyard (20:1-16)—yields much the same effect. Once again a contract is made for money, and once again it is broken in the name of generosity; yet once again there is at the end a reassertion of the claims of justice which have been violated, not by injustice, but by generosity itself. Here the problem is: How can I be generous to one person without being ungenerous to the next if I show only justice? Justice itself seems unjust if the system calls for generosity. The new mode of acting at one and the same time is an improvement on the old and a rejustification of it. In the householder's generosity we see a potential for both love and social chaos, while in his writing of contracts for pay we see his potential for both fairness and revenge. Apparently both the old order and the new are based on paradoxes, and the one needs the correction of the other. Not the establishment of one over the other, but the permanent tension of the two—that is what Jesus seems to envision as the way the old metaphors and the new should coexist.

Column D

But there is one more way Jesus approaches that problem. The passages in the fourth column show the approach at work. They show Jesus thoroughly at home with the metaphors which elsewhere he either changes, rejects, or replaces. Here he *accepts* them. Just as he pays the Temple tax and thereby operates completely within the system, so he thinks in the traditional terms and thereby operates completely within the system. He is even stricter about contracts, in particular the marriage contract, than Moses was (19:3-12), and he views God as primarily the repayer, the one who enforces the law (16:27). If he is hungry and the fig tree will not feed him, he will wither the tree in a gratuitous display of royal power (21:18-22); it is as though the tree has broken some sort of contract with Jesus, and must be repaid.

This episode with the tree is so bizarre but told so simply as though nothing were surprising about it that it is worth pausing over. Jesus' act is completely unintelligible unless it is seen as an example of what a king does to a wayward subject, an image then of what God will do to a wayward world. This is not the same Jesus as the one who spoke the first set of passages studied in this chapter. That Jesus valued the wayward sheep; this Jesus devastates the wayward tree.

Even just so, the householder in another parable (21:33-46), whose servants are beaten and whose son is killed by his tenants, confronts those tenants, certainly not to forgive them, not even just to kill them, but to "bring that wicked crowd to a bad end." And the king who in another parable (21:1-14) gave a wedding feast does not just forbid entrance to the improperly dressed man; he has him bound hand and foot and thrown into the darkness "to wail and grind his teeth." This is a king in the grand manner, yet Jesus says that "the kingdom of heaven may be compared" to this king's way of doing things. Jesus had once said that authority was for the sake of service, not majesty, but that is not what he is saying now.

The last words of Jesus' career, spoken before his trial and death, are a storm of images about the end of the world and the last judgment. There are four parts to the passage, and each one is a different version of this last encounter between himself and the rest of creation. For *he* is the "Son of Man" in the first passage (24:4-51), the bridegroom in the second (25:1-13), the man giving money to his servant in the third (25:14-30), and the judge of the universe in the last (25:31-46). The "Son of Man" comes, terrifying "in power and glory," to a shattered world; we are to estimate the dimensions of his power from the evidence of destruction and misery everywhere around him. The "bridegroom" comes in the night, and once again we see what his power means by looking upon the five foolish virgins who have had the door shut on them for a trivial fault. The "man going on a journey" seems lavish at first but has the mind of an extortionist who, reaping where he has not sown and gathering where he has not winnowed, throws his simple-minded and unresponsive servant into that same "outer darkness" to which an ever-increasing number of people are being consigned. And finally, the "judge" who comes in glory metes out rewards and punishments that are more than extravagant; they are *eternal*.

If they can be found anywhere in their pure form, the old metaphors of covenant, kingdom, and debt can be found pure in these four passages. Here the covenant is a contract of the most stringent kind that leads to the most terrible punishments; the royal power is of the most absolute and arbitrary kind, and the money transactions and the homage transactions are of the most impoverishing and humiliating kind for those with a debt to pay and a master to pay off. Jesus uses the old metaphors at their full force.

But there is one difference between the way he uses them and the way his forebears did. They used them to describe what the final meeting of *God* and the world would feel like. Jesus uses them to describe the world's meeting with *himself*. Here Jesus uses the old ideas in all their original meaning and emphasis, except that now they are no longer metaphors for God, but for himself. This is the ultimate metaphor: God-and-Jesus together are *the* king, *the* maker and breaker of human beings, *the* passer of laws and avenger of crimes, *the* source of all money and collector of all debts. At the very same time that Jesus thinks most in the old mode, he thinks least in it, violating it in its most sacred idea, the very idea under which he began his own ministry. That idea is the sovereign uniqueness of God. Yet here he himself takes all God's metaphors—the oldest, most awesome ones—and gives them to himself. Jesus set out to live under God as his father and thought of *father* as a word full of all good things. He seems to end acting more like a father than a son, and like a father of darker possibilities.

There is one passage in the long sequence of texts under consideration here which we still have not looked at. It is probably the most important of all. It is the passage dealing with the institution of the Eucharist (26:26-29). Nowhere is the rich complexity of Jesus' highly traditional yet highly individual way of living and thinking more abundantly demonstrated than here. The context is, of course, the feast of Passover, the commemoration of the meal eaten by the ancient Jews on the occasion of their liberation from Egypt. Jesus *accepts* completely the old feast and celebrates it completely. But in the midst of it, he also *changes* it, substituting for the blood of a lamb his own blood, and for the unleavened bread his own body. How much of a change is this? Is it merely an adjustment within the old idea? Yes. But is it also not too much of a change, so severe a change as to amount to a *rejection* of the old idea? The effect of the change is radically to invalidate the old meaning of the rite, to reduce it to the status of a preliminary symbol, an approximation or rough sketch of something immensely superior to it. When the painting is finished, the rough sketch is thrown away. But Jesus, who in the Eucharist *accepts* the old order, who *accepts but changes* it, and who both *changes and rejects* it, does one more thing to it: he *replaces* it. He simply takes its place. In the Eucharist, Jesus establishes the central rite of a new religion, and those who ever again will participate in it will participate also in his fourfold relationship to the old Temple and to the old metaphor of covenant, kingdom, and the payment of debts. By celebrating the Eucharist, his followers will enter into the heart of the fourfold paradox which is Jesus' life.

This, then, is what Jesus tried to do. He tried to rethink the life of God and humanity. To do that he had to rethink the metaphors that had already been used to give that life a structure and form. Toward that structure he assumed attitudes which logic would have forbidden as profoundly contradictory, but this was not to be an affair of logic. At the beginning it all seemed simple—a new metaphor (whether Temple or other image) replaced an old one which, therefore, was to be rejected. But that was not to be the whole story. The old Temple and the old images still spoke, still conveyed much. Revise them, then. Or—bolder still—take them at full force and make them your own. Let contradiction after contradiction confuse the enterprise at every turn, yet one thing is clear. To think about God, Jesus used every term and every strategy at his command, and at the end of the task we have, in the sheer magnitude and complexity of his effort, as good a measure as we can ever expect to have of how forever wrapped in mystery is God.

Jesus listened to the Pharisees telling him that in the past he could find the sanctioned truth of things. He also listened to Satan telling him that in himself he could find the sanction and the truth. At the beginning he rejected each of them. By the end he agreed with them both. Even they will have a place in his kingdom of paradox.

7. Image vs. Reality: The Failure of Jesus' Image of God

(Matthew 26:26—27:66)

The last of the paradoxes of Jesus' dilemma-ridden life is that metaphor itself is paradoxical because it is both an image of reality and a distortion, or, at best, an incomplete version of it. At the beginning the Pharisees had asserted their ancient metaphors as the very truth itself, and John had denounced the metaphors as a crowd of deceitful signs leading nowhere. Jesus would have to live out this paradox, too.

Father is not the same word as *God*. It is a "smaller" word. Its advantage is that it is more specific and concrete. Its disadvantage is that it is too specific and too concrete. The concept of *God* will stay inside the concept of *father* for a while, but not forever. He was *God* before he was *father* and, if he agrees to wear a fatherly aspect, it is not because he puts aside being *God*. Jesus eventually found the word *father* to be larger than he had originally thought it was, more full of both bright and dark dimensions. But no matter how complex and nuanced the word became, it was still smaller than that other word, *God*. Sooner or later, it would break apart under the strain of trying to contain a meaning too large for it.

This is the grandest example of what happens to all metaphors, even small ones. They all fail. They are, after all, the making equal of things that *are not equal*. They are all, then, literally false statements about reality. The fact that they are also the principal kind of statement human beings can make about the truth of things does not prevent them from being more deeply distortions and even betrayals of the truth. The world cannot be reduced to any metaphor we can impose upon it; nor can one's own self be reduced to the metaphors we have made up to help us cope with the world. *All metaphors fail.* In their failure the world and the self finally break clean and stand apart in their own unborrowed reality. That breaking apart is what happened to Jesus on the cross.

The only "plot" that can be extracted from the life of Jesus is, really, the story of what happens to his definition of God and of himself. He invested all his energies into that; outside of that, he can scarcely be said to exist for us. As a consequence, no ordinary historical biography or ordinary psychological analysis will ever be written about him. He vanishes utterly into the metaphors he has created to contain him and his God and his world. We can only see what happens to the metaphor.

The central metaphor of father and son was announced early and forcefully in three passages which have already received attention in this book. They are those of the Virgin Birth, the Baptism, and the "Our Father." Because they come so early and are so positive, there are in them only background hints of possible conflicts within the idea of father and son. In the Virgin Birth there was the *possibility* of conflict between human and divine birth. In the Baptism and Temptation there is the *possibility* of real conflict between or within the father and the son. And in the "Our Father" there is the *possibility* of a real split between the earth and heaven. All of these possible rifts remain obscure and remote at the beginning. Indeed, they were scarcely acknowledged as even possible. But each of them will be realized in turn.

The other passages which trace out the story of Jesus' principal metaphor are listed below. They are arranged in relation to the first three early passages we have just mentioned, since it seems to us that the later ones in effect comment on and develop the relatively simpler and more tranquil early passages. They bring to a crisis the conflicts latent there.

1. **The Virgin Birth**   1:18-25
   The Knowledge of Son and Father   11:25-27
   Jesus' New Family   12:46-50
   Jesus the Carpenter's Son   13:53-58
2. **The Baptism**   3:12-4:11
   First Prophecy of the Passion   16:21-23
   The Transfiguration   17:1-8
   (The Possessed Boy)   (17:14-18)
   Second Prophecy of the Passion   17:22-23
   Prayer to the Father   18:19-20
   Third Prophecy of the Passion   20:17-19

3.	The "Our Father"	6:9-13
	The Agony in the Garden	26:36-46
	The Trial of Jesus	26:57—27:31, esp. 26:63-64
	The Crucifixion	27:32-50, esp. 27:46

In the first group of texts, the first of the possible conflicts—that between a human and a divine birth—is realized. The early passage affirmed the union of these two things, in images which have since been summarized under the idea of the Virgin Birth. But the three later texts complicate the idea. Reading these three later texts in rapid and immediate succession gives one the unmistakable impression that the divine order and the human order do not share the same birth, nor do they even seem to want to. The first passage suggests a perfect intimacy between the divine father and his human son, the second a very real distinction between divine and earthly parentage, the third an open hostility between the two parental systems. The line goes straight from intimate to hostile, from compatible to polarized. Thus the conflict latent in the Virgin Birth is realized, and what had begun in harmony ends on the edge of violence.

In the second group of texts, the second of the possible conflicts—that between the father and the son themselves, quite apart from the rest of their "families"—is realized. The early passage had affirmed the harmony of father and son in the scene of the Baptism of Jesus. But the six later texts show that harmony to be badly strained. In this group are the three solemn announcements by Jesus that he will be put to death—by whom? for what? and how does he know?—and, in strongest possible contrast, there are the two other passages of the Transfiguration of Jesus and of his words on prayer. The Transfiguration is a kind of second Baptism, complete with the Father's repetition of the same words he had used before: "This is my beloved Son...." Jesus' later words on prayer amount to a reciprocal "This is my beloved Father." But how incongruous are these exchanges of love and confidence when they are seen sandwiched in between those others that talk of suffering and death! No matter how these things may be interpreted, something is out of plumb between the father and the son.

Another passage (17:14-18)—put in parentheses here because it does not formally belong to the sequence of texts now being discussed—throws an unexpected light on the puzzle. We have discussed earlier and will not repeat Jesus' exploration of the negative possibilities within the word *father.* The passage referred to here (17:14-18) is the only one in the gospel of Matthew which suggests a negative dimension to the word *son.* The father here is the kind of father that no doubt had led Jesus to take *father* as the entirely right word by which to know God. For the father is deeply sympathetic to his son's troubles, and does everything he can to provide for a cure. There is not the least sinister possibility in this father. But the son is altogether another story. We have seen many sick people in the gospel, but none who did what this son does. "For example, he often falls into the fire and frequently into the water." The son is the only self-destructive figure in the gospel. He is the one who does what Jesus had refused to do in the Temptations following the Baptism: "If you are the Son of God, *throw yourself down*" (4:5).

Is this what sons do? Jesus once asked rhetorically whether a father, asked for bread, would give his son a stone. The answer was supposed to be no, but he came to realize it might be yes. For the power of fatherhood is in giving and sustaining life, and the negative image of that power is the taking and murdering of life. The opposites are both made possible by the father's status as source of life. In the Baptism and Temptations, Jesus had affirmed the brighter side, not only of God as father, but also of himself as son. The positive aspect is grateful dependence on and loving homage to the father. But the boy who falls into the fire and the water shows the darker side of sons. That darkness is self-destruction. For the son is a being whose source is outside himself and whose characteristic act, insofar as he is *son* and only *son* and always *son,* is to deny himself in an affirmation of the other. The suicidal posture latent here is not of the usual kind where one directly intends to destroy oneself, but suicidal it nevertheless is. The second of those rifts possible from the very beginning—the one hidden but unacknowledged in the early scene of the Baptism and the Temptation—is thus realized. The darker possibility within the father is murder, within the son is suicide. As soon as the word is uttered, of course, it must be retracted. It was never the intention of the metaphor to lead to anything like this. When it does lead to this, it begins to collapse from within.

In the third group of texts under present consideration, we find the third and most awful potential conflict realized. It is the possibility of a conflict between the whole order of heaven as such and the whole order of earth as such. Our earliest text, that of Jesus' sublime prayer to "Our Father," looked to their unity, but further experience was to show that that unity existed mostly in hope and least in fact. The three later passages of dreadful majesty shatter the earlier hope.

In the Garden of Gethsemane Jesus experiences to the depths the utter loneliness of his position and the terror of the prospect facing him. The terrible emotions are there, and he turns them into a prayer to his father. At the outset of his career he had given his followers the "Our Father," and he continues that prayer here. "Thy will be done on earth as it is in heaven." Now he restates the original prayer in different words: "My Father, if it is possible, let this cup pass me by. Still, let it be as you would have it, not as I." The other prayer had gone on to ask for daily bread, for the forgiveness of debts, and for deliverance from evil. There is none of that now. Indeed, there is a premonition amounting to a certainty that the earlier prayer in its baldest form will *not* be answered. There will be no daily bread, nor deliverance from the evil to come. The Agony in the Garden is the scene in which the "Our Father" is rewritten. Jesus edits it to correct the impression left by the original version that God and human beings will perceive the human situation in the same ways. But Jesus has found that, pray for deliverance from evil as you will, God's definition of evil will not be yours. Pray for bread, but God will take *bread* in some other sense than yours. As for the forgiveness of debts, the metaphor of debts and payments and forgiveness has by now caused so much mischief that the meaning of the phrase is no longer clear, and its insertion into a prayer would serve no clear purpose. The "Our Father," then, is reduced to one phrase—"Thy will be done"—in which the key word, *will*, no longer refers to anything that can be defined in ways intelligible to people on earth.

In his trial Jesus maintains a complete silence except once to reassert that he is the son of God (26:63) and another time to reassert that he is the king of the Jews (27:11). He clings to his own metaphor, and clings also to the old Hebrew one he has inherited but recast for his own purposes. Whatever sonship and kingship may mean in this closing scene of his life, Jesus still is thinking in their terms. This is not the time to make new images for life nor to re-examine the ones which have become habitual. Jesus reasserts the ideas that have given shape and purpose to his life, and, because he cannot here do otherwise, reasserts them in a context that cannot make them seem to carry any clear meaning at all.

This is sonship? This is kingship?

The words cannot express what is happening here. The metaphors are being stretched too far.

Jesus is led out, whipped, crucified. At this extremity he utters one last prayer: "My God, my God, why have you forsaken me?" (27:46). It is the only time in the entire Gospel according to Matthew that Jesus calls him *God*. The last editing of the Lord's Prayer changes *our father* to *my God*. The larger word has broken out of the smaller, the less understandable out of the more understandable, the less human out of the more human, the cold out of the warm. The confident requests for a gracious paternal providence have changed to a single question which may be more accusation than question.

Once again Job raises his voice before the irrationality of God, except that for Job there was one less agony than for Jesus. Job did not have to give up the word that had held heaven and earth together for him. For Job, God was God. But for Jesus, God was father. For him to call on God rather than on the father, an outcome latent in the "Our Father" from the beginning of Jesus' career, at the end occupies the whole stage. Everything in this crucifixion scene gives only the sense of rending—the temple veil is torn, rocks are split—and heaven and earth, once joined by the idea that one was the father of the other, break apart. There are no father and son. There are only God and Jesus—heaven and earth—who see each other, if at all, across an abyss. Bridges to close the abyss have been built, but the abyss is wider than the bridges.

The promise of the Virgin Birth for the union of human and divine parentage, the promise of the Baptism and Temptations for the harmony of father and son, the promise of the "Our Father" for the community of heaven and earth all depended on one metaphor. And that metaphor is gone. The Pharisees had built metaphors across the abyss because one cannot live in the abyss. John had seen that the metaphors disguised but did not remove or fill up the abyss. By the end, Jesus embraced them both—both Pharisee and Baptizer, both the metaphor and the abyss.

Your Turn The abyss is never far away. Jesus experienced it in the shattering and falling of the central image that had, until the last moment, held the pieces of his life together. When the image was gone, so was the coherence of his life.

For this next exercise you will need some thirty index cards. First, take ten cards and on each of them write the name of one of your ten most important material possessions. Then arrange them in a straight line in an order from greatest to least value to you. Put the most important one closest to you, the least farthest away, with the others arranged in order between them.

Now put the cards on top of each other, the most important on the bottom, the least important on the top.

Look at the card on the top. Take time and think of yourself using and enjoying whatever is named there. Pick up the card and let it fall to the floor. Watch it fall. Allow yourself to be fully conscious of what it feels like to let this thing go.

Slowly repeat the process for each of the other nine cards. At the end, think of yourself without all these things. What is it like to let go of them all? With patience and care write out the answer to that question.

Take another ten cards. This time write on each card the name of one of the ten most important people in your life. Order the cards as above. Look at each card, slowly contemplate that person's importance to you, and drop the card to the floor. With each card's fall, allow yourself to be fully conscious of what it feels like to let this person go. At the end write down carefully and slowly what you have felt—about these people, about yourself, and about having let them all go.

Take another several cards. This time write on each of them the name of one of your "sub-personalities" which you identified in the exercise in Chapter 6. Fill more cards with other sub-personalities if you have discovered any more of them.

On the bottom of the stack place the one most important to you, on the top the one that is least important, and in between the others in order. Slowly look at each card, thinking of what you have invested in this sub-personality and what it has meant to you. One by one drop the cards to the floor. Again, allow yourself to be fully conscious of what it feels like to let this dimension of yourself go. After they are all gone, write down patiently and fully what it has felt like to let go of so much of yourself.

Now take one final card. You have let go of everything—things, people, identities. But there is one thing you still have not let go. That is your final identity as "The Observer" of all these other things, the one who chose them, the one who is at the center of them all.

What do you call this Observer? Write on the last card the name of this last "you." Reflect on it, feel its importance to you, and then drop the card to the floor just like all the others. Write what you feel about this last letting go.

When Jesus died he had been stripped of things, friends, and—no doubt most difficult of all—his sense of self, of identity, and of relationship to an ultimate and known center. The scene of his death is the image of everyone's.

You are asked, please, to keep all the cards you used in this exercise. We will need them for the exercise in the next chapter.

8. Jesus' New Image of God

(Matthew 28)

The last mention of money in the gospel of Matthew is almost the closing word. The chief priest and elders are said to bribe the guards to lie about Jesus' resurrection by claiming his body had been stolen. The world of money transactions, the world of contracts and agreements, discredits itself here once and for all. For whatever the resurrection of Jesus does or does not mean, it cannot be reduced to a plot after the manner of this world's plots.

Just what it means is, of course, difficult to establish. The notion of resurrection from the dead was certainly not invented for Jesus. It was a common belief among the so-called nature religions, based as they were on the death-and-resurrection cycle of the seasons. The idea of some sort of resurrection was familiar, too, in the Old Testament. Now and again a prophet raised up someone dead to show the power of God, as Jesus (in another gospel) also raised Lazarus. And Matthew himself seems to be deliberately underscoring the odd idea that, whatever else it may be, the resurrection of Jesus is not unique. For at the moment of Jesus' death, according to Matthew, "...tombs opened. Many bodies of saints who had fallen asleep were raised. ...they entered the holy city and appeared to many" (27:52-53). All this happens *before* Jesus is even buried. Jesus' own resurrection, then, does not happen without ample precedent.

The main difference between Jesus' resurrection and those others can be discerned in some of the brief and rather puzzling descriptive details which

Matthew includes in his account. There are, of course, the predictable bright light and earthquake to go with the opening of heaven—the kind of descriptive detail we have seen before in the Baptism and the Transfiguration. But this time those things are said to accompany an angel, not Jesus. Even all this panoply and fanfare are not unique to Jesus. If neither resurrection nor divine glory and power as such is presented as unique to Jesus, what *is?*

Matthew presents, without comment, the details which obliquely suggest what is unique here. He has the angel say once and Jesus himself say a second time that the disciples are to go to Galilee. More specifically, Jesus, in a direction alluded to but not directly quoted (28:16), tells them to go to a particular mountain in Galilee. It apparently is not important for us to know which mountain. Once everyone is gathered there, Jesus delivers the briefest of the major speeches of his career, all of two verses long. In it he tells his followers to make disciples of all nations.

Galilee, a mountain, and a speech. A scene is being set, with as much attention to symbolic and metaphorical effect as by now we should expect from Jesus and the gospel of Matthew. Galilee is the place where Jesus came from in the first place. And mountains are the places where on key occasions new revelations come from: on Sinai the Law, on another mountain the Beatitudes. Galilee and mountains—the places of beginnings. It is an inaugural scene, and the brief speech Jesus gives there is an inaugural address. That is what makes Jesus' resurrection unique. The others are taken as displays of divine power or as the cyclical rebirth of nature. But this one is taken for a beginning of something that was not there before. But what is being inaugurated? The clues must be in Jesus' address: what is in that speech that was not there before? 'Full authority has been given to me both in heaven and on earth; go, therefore, and make disciples of all the nations. Baptize them in the name "of the Father, and of the Son, and of the Holy Spirit." Teach them to carry out everything I have commanded you. And know that I am with you always, until the end of the world!' (28:18-20)

Jesus' authority was there before, though perhaps not so explicitly conceived as universal. Seeking converts was there before, though again not as so universal an enterprise. Baptism, of course, was there before. The Father and the Son were there—theirs was, in fact, the whole story. What was not there before, except for the briefest glimpse, was the Holy Spirit. The Spirit was said to have been responsible for Mary's pregnancy, and was said to have descended upon Jesus in the form of a dove at his Baptism, and was said to have led him into the desert to be tempted afterwards. But that is all. Yet here the Holy Spirit—whatever that name means—is mentioned in the same breath and with the same emphasis as the Father and the Son. *That* is what is new here. We have a new metaphor for God.

And, whatever it may mean, it must be a metaphor of surpassing importance. In his one earlier statement concerning the Spirit in Matthew's gospel, Jesus had said: "That, I assure you, is why every sin, every blasphemy, will be forgiven men, but blasphemy against the Spirit will not be forgiven" (12:31). As though to make sure there would be no misunderstanding, Jesus immediately added: "Whoever says anything against the Son of Man will be forgiven, but whoever says anything against the Holy Spirit will not be forgiven, either in this age or in the age to come" (12:32). He gives the Spirit some kind of preeminence over the Son and by implication, since the Son exists wholly in reference to the Father, over the Father as well. In this last metaphor of the gospel we have also the last paradox of the gospel. There is something more sacred than the Son, more sacred therefore than the Father of the Son—not just as sacred, but more.

The original terms of Jesus' metaphor must therefore be taken to have been by themselves an inadequate statement about God. We have seen that, both because of the negative or darker dimensions of the concept of father and son, and because of the inability of even the most positive metaphor to exhaust the reality of its referent, the task of naming God and defining God was impossible from the beginning. So was the task of naming or defining the relationship of human beings to him. Therefore that Jesus *did* define both God and himself as Father and Son does not prevent those metaphors from being, like all metaphors, *literally false* statements about reality. To take any metaphor as *literally* true is an act of madness and a betrayal of the truth. The impact of the crucifixion on Jesus' original metaphor was to force a recognition that whatever is meant by *father* and *son* among human beings is only approximately true, true in a manner of speaking, true from a certain angle, true tentatively, true remotely about God. It may be the best statement possible, but it is still not an adequate statement.

The new metaphor of the Spirit corrects the overstatement in the older one about fathers and sons. It gives a different notion of God, at once antithetical and complementary to the other one. Where *father* and *son* are altogether definite and even confining, *spirit* is indefinite and liberating. Where *father* and *son* refer to a cause-and-effect relationship, *spirit* refers to something vague, mysterious, unpredictable, unstable—even accidental, if that is not too strong a word. Where *father* and *son* imply a hierarchical relationship stabilized by providence on the one side and obedient homage on the other, *spirit* implies relationships that never stabilize, that are always being arbitrarily revised.

For the word *spirit* means *wind*.

That is the new metaphor for God that comes out of the resurrection of Jesus. In it is his resurrection.

Even in our own day, it is true to say that the wind operates by no known laws. Weather forecasters have at best a general sense of what the wind will do even a day from now, and this in spite of their ability, thanks to space technology, to get outside the weather and look down on it. If the wind is still a vagabond element when seen from that high vantage point, it must have seemed the wildest force of nature to the ancient Jews, who first saw it as an emblem of God. Often they took storms to be an emblem of God, but in their minds it was not just storms that resembled him. It was also the cool breeze of the evening. It was hot blasts and cold ones and the temperate breezes, too. Precisely because of its ambiguity, its lack either of a clear point of origin or a clear destination; because of its ability to refresh the sun-tortured person and its ability to reduce jagged rock to smooth contours; because of people's inability to understand it and their great ability to feel it—precisely, then, because of its character as an affront to logic and to language—the ancient Jews saw in it an emblem of God. Indeed, the Old Testament did more than prohibit by law the making of graven images. Through the idea of *spirit* it also qualified and purged—though it never prohibited—*any* too definite image of God whatever, including any metaphor that seemed too stable or intelligible. The better the metaphor, the more dangerous, because too easily taken for adequate and true. If all the other metaphors, including *father* and *son*, give God a definition, the metaphor of *wind* gives him back his freedom from definitions.

In the crucifixion the breakdown of the older metaphor is experienced in an inexhaustible tragedy. In the resurrection it is re-experienced in an attitude of delight. The older metaphor is not buried; it is simply corrected by another one that celebrates another principle. *From one point of view it is terrible that all the words fail; from another there is nothing more pleasing than that both God and humanity are larger than–in any case, other than–the formulas that try to contain them.* The crucifixion shows that that is terrible, the resurrection that it is wonderful.

Tens of thousands of years before Jesus—and before Moses, for that matter—another group of people seem to have come close to this idea. They were the Cro-Magnon, among the earliest true human beings. On the walls of caves in France and Spain they painted rather than wrote their thoughts. But in their pictures they did what the Bible does, what Matthew's gospel does. They established metaphors by which to define the meaning of their lives. The images they have left—of splendid horses and bison, proud goats, gentle deer, powerful serpents and seals, delicate plants—tell what was vivid and clear for them about their lives. These were the normal terms. Scientists do not yet know if these images were used in magical rites or whether something totemistic is implied in them. But we do not need to know precisely the meaning of each form to understand that in these images the first human beings were saying what it felt like to them to be alive. The sense of a surging world of life, of seasons and hunting, of beauty and the needs of survival, is too powerful in these images to be an accident.

But these earliest people have left another set of images behind. This second set of metaphors on the walls of caves says *the other thing* about what life felt like to them. The images are called "meanders," or more colorfully, "macaronis." They were not made by paints. They were made by the fingertips tracing what look like doodles into the soft clay of the caves. They are done sometimes with a single finger, sometimes with two, three, or four. Great swirls of them sweep around the caves, done, it seems, by several people at once—and perhaps many people at once. They cross over and under each other, twist around obstacles in the wall, sometimes squiggle, sometimes proceed in straight lines and then abruptly turn and go off in loops or waves. In their bison and deer these more-than-ancient people left behind one statement about life. In their "macaronis" they left *the other one*. Which is the more exuberant it is impossible to say—and meaningless to ask. They felt life both ways, and said so.

The gospel of Matthew ends with *the other statement* about God and humanity, and their life together. It is the same affirmation, made in incredibly more elaborate and sophisticated form, as that made at the very beginning of the life of the modern human. If life is the bison and deer, it is also the "macaronis." If it is fathers and sons, it is also the wind. If it is sometimes captured, it is nevertheless always free. If it is sometimes defined, it still is everywhere a mystery. If it is sometimes a project with purposes and goals and proper and improper behaviors, it is also a thing of whimsy and charm. If it is urgent and tragic, it is also funny.

It is not enough to baptize anyone into the Father and the Son. Matthew ends his gospel with Jesus himself saying that is not enough. It will be enough only when all the nations have been baptized also into The Wind. Otherwise, all the metaphors by which people seek to say what their lives are all about would have only a kind of Calvary as their final implication—in other words, only a death.

Your Turn   But our discussion so far might make it seem as though the wind has no function other than to confuse everything by robbing everything of its initial clarity. And that, indeed, seems at first sight to be true. For example, light a candle in a still dark room and let it burn until the flame stands steady. Then very gently blow some smoke toward the flame. Until it gets to the flame the smoke seems to have a fairly simple shape. Once it gets to the flame, though, it turns in many directions at once, and loses itself in the many currents of what would have to be called a mild wind. What is the wind doing here to the smoke?

Is it a source of disorder—or is it the source of some new kind of order? Write what you think.

Or try another simple experiment with the "wind." This time boil some water in a pan—for the currents of water and those of the air behave very similarly—and drop into it a single letter from some alphabet soup. Watch carefully how the letter moves—first, in a gentle curling motion from top to bottom and back again, and second in a clockwise or counterclockwise direction around the walls of the pan. What do you think the "wind" is doing? *Why* all this apparently random movement?

Fold several ice cubes in a cloth and hold them to one side of the pan and watch what happens to the "winds" in the water as they move the letter around. Now suddenly dump the ice cubes into the water and watch again. What happens to the letter between now and when the water boils again?

Surely what you have just seen is not without order. It will happen more or less the same way every time you do it. But what is the order, the logic, of the wind? Does this shapeless thing have, after all, a predictable structure?

Of course it does, and you have just seen that structure with your own eyes. The purpose of the wind is to balance opposite forces against each other.

In the candle flame the heat of the fire and the coldness of the surrounding air were constantly balancing off each other. The smoke you blew into the flame merely enabled you to see what was already happening as the cold and heat reacted to each other.

The same is true of the letter of alphabet soup—it enabled you to see what was happening anyway. The bottom of the pan was hot and the top relatively cool, so the letter went around in an up-and-down circular movement. One side of the pan was relatively hot and another relatively cool, so the noodle went around and around horizontally, almost as though looking for a spot to sit still, where everything would be in balance. When you put the ice cubes into the pan you slowed the action down, that's all.

The winds you have watched had one function only—to balance off the opposite forces that were at work within the system. They brought the heat to the cold, and the cold to the heat; left to right, right to left; what was going up to what was going down. The wind is the reconciler of opposites, the resolver of paradoxes.

Here is the opening sentence of the Bible. Notice that the "wind" is already there even before God gave the world its final shape: "In the beginning, when God created the heavens and the earth, the earth was a formless wasteland, and darkness covered the abyss, while a mighty wind swept over the waters." (Gen. 1:1-2)

How many pairs of opposites do you find explicitly or implicitly contained even in this simple passage?

We find these: the earth and abyss (or sea), heaven (up) and earth (down), and left and right (the wind sweeping from one side to the other). Also the "darkness" is the beginning of a pair of opposites which will include the "light."

Here is the rest of the Bible's first account of creation: "Then God said, 'Let there be light,' and there was light. God saw how good the light was. God then separated the light from the darkness. God called the light 'day,' and the darkness he called 'night.' Thus evening came, and morning followed—the first day.

"Then God said, 'Let there be a dome in the middle of the waters, to separate one body of water from the other.' And so it happened: God made the dome, and it separated the water above the dome from the water below it. God called the dome 'the sky.' Evening came, and morning followed—the second day.

"Then God said, 'Let the water under the sky be gathered into a single basin, so that the dry land may appear.' And so it happened: the water under the sky was gathered into its basin, and the dry land appeared. God called the dry land 'the earth,' and the basin of the water he called 'the sea.' God saw how good it was. Then God said, 'Let the earth bring forth vegetation: every kind of plant that bears seed and every kind of fruit tree on earth that bears fruit with its seed in it.' And so it happened: the earth brought forth every kind of plant that bears seed and every kind of fruit tree on earth that bears fruit with its seed in it. God saw how good it was. Evening came, and morning followed—the third day.

"Then God said: 'Let there be lights in the dome of the sky, to separate day from night. Let them mark the fixed times, the days and the years, and serve as luminaries in the dome of the sky to shed light upon the earth.' And so it happened: God made the two great lights, the greater one to govern the day and the lesser one to govern the night; and he made the stars. God set them in the dome of the sky, to shed light upon the earth, to govern the day and the night, and to separate the light from the darkness. God saw how good it was. Evening came, and morning followed—the fourth day.

"Then God said, 'Let the water teem with an abundance of living creatures, and on the earth let birds fly beneath the dome of the sky.' And so it happened: God created the great sea monsters and all kinds of swimming creatures with which the water teems, and all kinds of winged birds. God saw how good it was, and God blessed them, saying 'Be fertile, multiply, and fill the water of the seas; and let the birds multiply on the earth.' Evening came, and morning followed—the fifth day.

"Then God said, 'Let the earth bring forth all kinds of living creatures: cattle, creeping things, and wild animals of all kinds.' And so it happened: God made all kinds of wild animals, all kinds of cattle, and all kinds of creeping things of the earth. God saw how good it was. Then God said: 'Let us make man in our image, after our likeness. Let them have dominion over the fish of the sea, the birds of the air, and the cattle, and over all the wild animals and all the creatures that crawl on the ground.'

"God created man in his image; in the divine image he created him; male and female he created them.

"God blessed them, saying: 'Be fertile and multiply; fill the earth and subdue it. Have dominion over the fish of the sea, the birds of the air, and all the living things that move on the earth.' God also said: 'See, I give you every seed-bearing plant all over the earth and every tree that has seed-bearing fruit on it to be your food; and to all the animals of the land, all the birds of the air, and all the living creatures that crawl on the ground, I give all the green plants for food.' And so it happened. God looked at everything he had made, and he found it very good. Evening came, and morning followed—the sixth day.

"Thus the heavens and the earth and all their array were completed. Since on the seventh day God was finished with the work he had been doing, he rested on the seventh day from all the work he had undertaken." (Gen. 1:3—2:3)

What other pairs of opposites do you find here?

We find these: light and darkness, water above and water below, land and sea, dry land and seed, night and day, nonliving and living, sea life and land life, nature and human, male and female, and finally work and rest. Everything is created in pairs of opposites, so that nothing exists unless it is balanced off against something else. Everything exists, then, in a vital, dynamic relationship with its opposite. Common sense shows us this is true of the paired opposites of male and female, but further reflection shows the same principle holds literally for *everything*: there is no left without a right, there is no up without a down, no warmth without a mixture of cold and hot, and so on.

The whole system of creation, then, is pictured as simply a more elaborate version of what you saw in your pot of boiling water.

And what is the force that brings all the opposites together—that brings hot and cold, up and down, left and right into a single dynamic relationship? It is the same force you saw at work in the candle and on the stove: the "wind."

The Bible begins by ascribing to the wind the work of reconciling the opposites, and the gospel of Matthew ends with Jesus giving it the same function for a more complicated world.

Indeed, before "the wind" is called on to reconcile the opposites within the world at large, it is called on to reconcile them within God himself. We have seen that the metaphor of father and son, which started off being so harmonious, ended by being utterly polarized. What had looked like a symphony of similar natures turned increasingly into a tension of opposite ones. The first work of the wind, then, is to bring these opposites together again. It is to give to the father something of the son and to the son something of the father. If the wind did not "circulate" within the Godhead itself in much the same way it circulates over the land and sea and from equator to poles, there would be no more life in God than there would be on the planet earth. The role of the wind is that simple and that basic.

Christian theology has long acknowledged the role of the "wind" even within the life of God by declaring that an essential part of the definition of God is that he is, not only the Father and not only the Son, but also the Spirit-Wind that moves between them and makes them one. The ancient doctrine of the Trinity reflects the idea that there have to be three metaphors, not just one or two, for God; and that the third, that of the wind, is the one that makes a unity of what otherwise would be "irreconcilable" opposites.

In the closing exercise of our study of the images of Jesus in the gospel of Matthew, we invite you to explore how the Spirit-Wind might move through your life as it does through the life of creation and even through the life of God. For the final gift of Jesus to the world was this last, billiant metaphor of the Wind.

Clear a large space on the floor around you. In large bright letters write each of the following words on each of six index cards: Hot, Cold, Light, Dark, Male, Female. Arrange the cards in a large circle on the floor so that the opposite qualities are physically opposite to each other, thus:

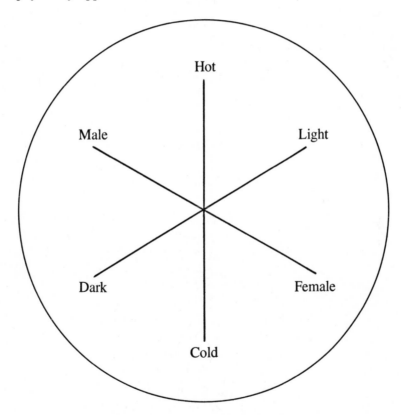

Take the thirty or so cards you used in the exercise in the last chapter and very carefully decide where on this circle each one should go. The various categories of hot, light, etc., are of course being used metaphorically here, so that, for example, one's spouse need not be too literally classified under "male" or "female"—but might better be classified as "light" or "cold," etc., depending on whether he or she is *like* "light" or "cold" to you. In order to classify all your cards, you therefore first have to decide for yourself what each of the categories means to you *metaphorically*.

What feelings do you associate with each of them?

Light

Dark

Hot

Cold

Male

Female

Now you are ready to put each of your cards into one of these categories. Lay each of them on the floor nearest to the category you think it most resembles.

Stand in the center of the circle. Look at each set of cards in turn, and then move toward one of them. *You are the Wind.*

Stand above the first set of cards and see what each of the things clustered there has in common with the others. Then slowly move back across the center and toward the opposite cluster. Move back and forth as often as you need to in order to sense how important these opposites are to each other. You, in your role as the wind, are bringing them together. What does it mean to say that you are bringing them together?

Now repeat the same procedure for each of the other two sets of paired opposites. What do you bring together in the second set?

And in the third set?

You have followed the Wind in several small circles of its movement:

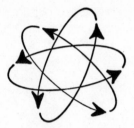

But the Wind blows also in a great circle that embraces everything. Walk with the Wind in that great circle now. Stand at any point on your circle and walk slowly to the next and to the next until you have gone all the way around. You, the Wind, are bringing unity into all these different things. You bring something from the "dark" to the "hot," from the "hot" to the "male," and so on. They are no longer separate. You are bringing them together. All the many dimensions of your life are seen now as involved in each other, unified, complementary, necessary, whole. You are a universe. Reflect on your work as the unifying and reconciling Wind, and write what your work is accomplishing in your world.

And finally, do what Genesis says God did on the last day of his work. Having roamed like the Wind over all parts of his world, he returned to his own place and rested. Go back to the center of your circle. Stop the roaming and stand still. From the quietness of that center—from the peace of that Sabbath rest—do what God did. For "God looked at everything he had made, and he found it very good."

With the help of that last image Jesus gave us for God, you have made the circle of your life. We invite you now to write for yourself the closing passage of this book. From the center of your circle write about what you see. We make only one suggestion, that you make this your first sentence:

"I look at everything I have made, and I find it very good."